Dedication

This book is dedicated to Steve and AJ, who encouraged my writing and to every Social Worker who will or is now working in nursing homes. Rock on.

Preface

Empathy: the action of understanding, being aware of, being sensitive to, and vicariously experiencing the feelings, thoughts, and experience of another of either the past or present without having the feelings, thoughts, and experience fully communicated in an objectively explicit manner; http://www.merriam-webster.com/dictionary/empathy

So you think the word 'home' in nursing home is true do you? Well for most places, I'm afraid not. Nursing homes have plenty of rules; just piss off staff, especially on the evening and night shift and see how fast they are enforced. Evening and night shift staff work these hours for a reason; they think they won't have to do much.

1) You hear at the care plan meeting you can have snacks and/or tea or coffee anytime. Translation of 'ok, sure' is usually 'we will see if there is any instant decaf in the

nurse's kitchenette or tea bags, but don't hold your breath. You thought it took a long time to help you with the bathroom, just wait and see how long it takes for a snack or beverage. Staff will always sound nice at care plan meetings telling you: 'sure, you can have those in the evening, just have to ask.' Of course, in your own home you were able to have a kitchen to use whenever you liked.

2) You are not tired yet? It's 8:00PM and you should be in bed, according to staff. They will just have to make out a behavior sheet for the Social Service Department because you won't go to bed on time. Oh, you're not 10 years old and have no place urgent to be in the morning? Staff doesn't care. But, remember we will get you up at 5:30AM for our (staff) convenience. Didn't know getting old was going to be like a job, did you?

Welcome Home! But more like: "Abandon hope all ye who enter here".....Divine Comedy

Introduction

When I was growing up, empathy was taught in my home to us. I remember being brought to task more than once by my mother concerning the meaning of empathy. It was usually when she would catch me being mean to another kid, or making a disparaging remark about someone in the store who looked different than me. She would take me aside and ask me how I thought I might feel if I were in the other person's shoes. After a mild tongue lashing, I was told to just sit and reflect on other peoples' feelings for a while. Many of my friends displayed empathy back then, for those who didn't display it we would often discuss how we felt sorry for them because their parents didn't care enough to teach it to them.

I am concerned because somehow, over the years, in America, empathy has faded and it has faded to the point of being seen as something to avoid for fear we will be looked upon as weak. Most people in our modern society no longer seem to give a damn about what other people believe, feel, say or like and being rude has become the new norm but America has not always been this callous toward one another.

The Great Depression of the 1930's ushered in a President who created programs so that older Americans wouldn't be left to starve once their working years were ended. President Roosevelt understood back then that many elderly were starving and homeless after working for ungrateful companies all of their adult lives, many had sacrificed a great deal, not only for their jobs, but for their country as well. That was a time in our country's history that America, as a whole, felt empathy for each other.

Over the years corporations have grown stronger and the empathy that used to be felt by Americans for others has grown weaker, especially in the area of respect for elderly people. As the number of elderly in America has grown, along with our mounting concern of the bottom line, the elderly are no longer valued in any way, shape or form like they were when their population was much lower, as in previous generations. In fact, our country's obsession with the corporate bottom line has given birth to the more prevalent value of greed, so much so that greed now outweighs most any other value Americans used to hold dear. This new century seems to have spawned the notion that when things don't get done, everyone is to blame, but ourselves, and we have a new cry throughout the land: "We are not our brother's keeper."

Greed has takeen our nation's economy to a low that has not been seen since the Great Depression of the 1930's so lately, we are finding that greed and destruction of other values obviously is not working. America is seeing a division of political party lines, the likes of which haven't been seen since the nation was divided by the Civil War of the United States in the 18 hundreds. Since none of the above scenarios appear to be functioning well for America, maybe it's time Americans once again learned empathy and how to care about our fellow human beings, not just towards people of some foreign country, but towards people within our own great nation.

I first became very aware of how a great deal of the elderly felt about living in a nursing home years ago when I became a Nursing Assistant. As an Assistant my tasks included making sure the elderly were clean, fed and able to get to activities and therapy sessions as needed along with answering call bells when they rang for help. We Aides always had numerous tasks to perform and many residents to care for in our eight hour shifts and since we were usually over booked, so to speak, this seldom left us with much time to be able to sit down and talk to the residents at any great length, but once in a while, when bathing or showering a resident, I was able to listen a bit longer to some of them.

I would hear a few tales from various residents about how proud they were of their families but, more often than not, I would hear tales of sadness. Tales that said far too many were not very content with their situations, but more to the point, unhappy with how nursing homes did things and how they were set up and run. Stories of how the routine showers were few and far between and they often felt like they were being run through a car wash when they finally did get showers and eating the main dining room felt more like eating in a military mess hall, which did little to stimulate appetite. One of the biggest complaints, from almost everyone able to express their thoughts, was a concerned having to get up in the morning at five or six every day and as one gentleman put it: "I am old, retired and I got up every day for 50 years at six in the morning, where in the hell am I going now to have to get up so early?" and I must say he had a good point.

Since those Nurse Aide days, I have obtained a BA degree and continued to work with the elderly first as an Activity Director in a nursing home, then as a Case Manager in the community and most recently as a Social Services Director in nursing homes. The message from many of the elderly residing in nursing homes has remained the same; they do not feel at home in a nursing home.

In our modern society the idea being accepted by the public is; nursing homes work well and someone has to care for our aging population somehow. As an insider, working with the elderly for many years, I'm here to tell you that message does not ring true; not to the people living in a nursing home.

While it is true that many elderly in traditional nursing homes in the past and many in the present, have adapted to conditions in those places, especially those people who grew up during the Depression Era, and are able to put up with certain things in those places as they exist right now, but no one should have to tolerate inconveniences, give up their

❈

individuality, or live by arbitrary rules just because they have grown old and need some help with daily routines.

Nursing homes all put forth a good façade, every single one of them have their tours, their folders and their pamphlets showing families the benefits of nursing home life for their loved ones, should they choose to place the loved ones in their care. Every nursing home is quick to display those pamphlets, which are typically graced with pictures of an elderly resident smiling, usually with the arm of one of the staff members draped around their shoulders. Pictures placed there for marketing purposes and designed to maintain their credibility with the public. This form of advertising is used, most often by corporate owned nursing homes, to give families the illusion or perception that the facility in the picture is a beautiful place to live when old. The false impression being presented to the public conveys the message that each individual living in that facility is important and everyone's distinctive needs are met. After all, who knows more about the power of propaganda in advertising than corporations? Corporations are, for the most part, a vast enterprise in salesmanship. All of these things are designed to disguise the flaws that exist within traditional nursing homes.

I became very interested about the quality life for people in nursing homes because the Sociologist in me wanted to understand how residents felt about life within those walls and why so many people fear living in them and for a long time Sociologist have tended to ignore the problems older people face in traditional nursing homes; not considering the issue to be very important. The more I worked with the elderly, the more I heard from them and their families, that nursing home issues are quite important to them.

I feel that the powerful messages, being conveyed and advertised by and sent forth by nursing homes, plus the need that exists within our society for caring professionals to look after our elderly loved ones when we are unable to do so at home, are worthy of an investigation by one and all.

This is not to say all hope is lost if someone you love must go to a nursing home. I am writing this book because there is a big change taking place in some of the finest nursing homes in America. It is called Culture Change, and while it is wonderful, unfortunately those places where culture change has replaced the old institutional model which was concerned with just getting tasks done in an efficient manner, by a more individualized approach, where residents' personal and individual habits and tastes are in the front position, making them more like home, are, right now, a very small number. I am also writing this book because every nursing home in the country can, and should, redesign their way of thinking. It can be done but it will take the efforts of not just very caring leaders running the nursing home industry, but also the determined efforts of people who have loved ones in those places, joining together saying: "This is not acceptable and we demand changes."

All through this book I talk often about St. Barley's, the most recent nursing home where I was a Social Service Director, the name of the nursing home and people in it have been changed to protect their privacy. I use St. Barley's as an example throughout, because it pretty much pinpoints how the typical nursing home is run today, and how most have been run, for a very long time now, while in other areas it is unique but not always in a good way. I am hoping to give you, a very accurate look at how it feels to live in a traditional nursing home. I want you, the reader, to understand what it's like down to your very soul and I am hoping it will be an eye-opener and that you will agree it is time for every facility in America to change for the good of all people living in one.

Table of Contents

Do not go gentle into that good night,

Old age should burn and rave at close of day;

Rage, rage against the dying of the light.

Dylan Thomas

Nursing Homes can be bad For Your Health and Wellbeing

I knock on the door of Room 103 saying: "Hello, may I come in?" I peer around the door after hearing nothing. I knock again and wait, still no answer. I open the door a crack and see an elderly lady sitting on the edge of her bed in the room. I say, again: "May I come in?" a bit louder, in case she is hard of hearing. The lady looks up at the door: "Do whatever you want," . I slowly enter the room. I am smiling, I identify myself and I ask the lady if I might ask her a few questions. "What for?" is her response. "We ask everyone some basic questions when they first come in. It helps us get to know new people, it is required by The State and it goes in your medical chart." She looks at me, head lowered and the look appears suspicious, like she doesn't believe me. I clear my throat and try to continue the conversation by saying: "Welcome to St. Barley's." She raises her head a bit, "Go to Hell," is what I get. Not quite the reply I expected from this frail looking person, but I am not surprised by her response as it is not the first time I have heard it from a resident, even though this is my first week at St. Barley's Nursing Home and Rehab. I try the first question anyway. "What was your mother's first name?" I ask her. She replies but in a tone that lets me know she is not happy with answering. I try the next question: "What was your father's name?" Now she lowers her head again, peers up at me through squinted eyes and asks me: "Do you like this job?" I answer: "Yes, I do. I like Social Work very much." "Why?" is her next question. I have asked myself the same question especially since working at St. Barley's, but I try to give her the sincerest answer I can. "I like to help people and this job is a good way to do it," I answer. "Can you get me out of here then?" She asks me, with tears welling up in her eyes. "You have only been here one day," I say to her, "You dislike us already?" She looks at me again, this time tears streaming down her face and says: "I want to go home, this place is not my home it never will be my home." "Do you understand?" I understand all too well what her words are saying to me.

Her words make me think back, years ago, before I went to college, about my own mother, who was elderly and became very sick. My family and my father had vowed my mother would never be assigned to a traditional nursing home, if we could ever help it. There were eight of us kids and we took turns helping my father care for my mom when she became too sick to care for herself. She did, eventually, go into a nursing home, but she was out of it, so to speak, and pretty much in a coma when the ambulance came to take her to the hospital, then to a nursing home. She was comatose so I am sure she would forgive us at that point, for our decision. But what about the people who are simply frail, but their minds are still there? Those people, who are aware, fear nursing homes because they fear losing the simplest things in life that we, living on the outside, take for granted. Being able to make even the simplest decisions, are often taken away in nursing homes. Nursing homes are not evil places, run by evil people. In fact, nursing homes have the best of intentions, but like the saying goes: "The road to Hell is paved with good intentions." Good intentions are not enough to keep one's quality of life at a level where they can be happy. My mom had always made us promise to never put her into one of 'those places,' as she liked to call them.

I turn my attentions back to Mary, the lady in Room 103 whom I am trying to interview. "I'm not a miracle worker," I reply, "But I can set up a care plan meeting with the team here and with you and your family so we can discuss why you are unhappy. Maybe we can all work something out that you would be happy with." Now Mary has the first faint look of hope on her face since our conversation began. "I cannot promise anything, Mary, but I can try for a care plan meeting." She gives me a half smile and stops crying, for now anyway. "I will come back later, if you like, to ask these questions, when you are feeling better." She looks at me, once again and says: "Maybe tomorrow, after breakfast," she says as more of a question than a reply. "It's a date then," I say as I gather up my papers and clipboard and head for the door. I feel tears welling up in my own eyes, I want to hug Mary and say: "Things will be ok," but I know things may not be ok, at least not to her satisfaction anyway. I cannot imagine a worse way to spend my final days of old age, having to live in a traditional nursing home, sharing my bedroom with a virtual stranger and having to get used to rules in a place that is categorically an institution.

I return to the Social Work office, "How did your first interview here go?" the Social Services Director asks me. "Not real well, she hates it here," I answer. "Many people do," is the answer the Director gives me, smiling, but with a pained look, telling me she fully understands why.

Crystal, the Social Services Director is all of 26 years old, but she has an understanding of people, especially the elderly, that goes way beyond her 26 years. She is a very good Director, but I also know, from the first time we met, she is not happy working at St. Barley's anymore lately. When I had asked her why, she said it was a fine job until the new Administrator was hired and then everything seemed to change. When I asked her if maybe change is hard to adjust to, she told me, no, change is fine with her. But she said she gets the distinct feeling that Madeline, the new

Administrator, hates her guts for some reason. I knew pretty much, from meeting the Administrator during my interview, that Madeline was no touchy, feely sort of boss. I got the feeling, after just one week on the job, that Madeline didn't seem to like anyone much. She was an efficient, cool as a cucumber, sort of Administrator who felt the authoritarian type of supervisors got the job done more efficiently. The woman was not oozing with massive people skills. She was the kind of Administrator who relished in her authority over people and she shot down anyone who dared disagree with her. Her favorite habit, for keeping the staff in line, was to call out people in our morning staff meetings, those she felt 'don't get it' or who just plain tick her off for some reason. She enjoyed embarrassing staff, be they nurses, Social Services, food service, maintenance, just anyone who makes her mad. She has the kind of personality (some circles may call it bi-polar) that makes it impossible to know what will tick her off, so all staff members were usually on edge all the time because of it. In fact one day in morning meeting, the Maintenance Assistant was filling in for the head maintenance person and said something the Administrator didn't like. She had asked him what was going to be done about some mechanical problem in one of the resident's rooms and apparently the Administrator didn't like his answer. The Administrator all of a sudden raised her voice and proceeded to bust the poor guy's balls over the subject. She ranted and raved, telling him he was an idiot, for about a good 15 minutes. Everyone in the meeting, especially the maintenance guy, seemed stunned by this craziness. The guy looked like he might be going to cry or something, he looked very upset. The entire staff appeared to be embarrassed for the poor guy and it didn't start anyone's day with a cheerful note. As it turned out, he had been much more upset than anyone realized and a few days later, the head maintenance woman came into Social Services crying her eyes out. "What's wrong?" I asked her. "Charlie is dead," she sobbed. "What?" I asked her, in a stunned voice. "Charlie is dead," she repeated. "Did he have some kind of accident?" I inquired. "No, he shot himself in the head," she wailed. I just couldn't believe my ears. Charlie must have had some crap going on in his personal life and his getting chewed out by the Administrator probably was the straw that broke the camel's back. To say this woman was Attila the Hun in a dress is a gross understatement. Compassion was not

Madeline's big suit either. Her personality suited the owner of St. Barley's though because whatever she lacked in people skills, she more than made up for in number crunching and saving him money to make him richer. Her personality would have been best suited as an accountant or a person who worked with computers, in a cubicle where she could be alone and not have to deal with people, but definitely not an administrator. Madeline also had her little snitches, her rats, her patsies, whatever you want to call them, whom she often met with to find out information or the dirt on other workers. This kind of work environment did little to encourage cooperation among staff members. In fact, driving a wedge between co-workers was more this Administrator's style, making for a pretty stressful place to work every day. Maybe she worried that the staff might become friends and mutiny or something, against her one day. Maybe the fear of losing one's job just suited her by keeping everyone off balance. It seems ludicrous but her favorite speech to staff was about team work. I think she liked this because it was a nice buzz word and it probably made her feel like she was encouraging everyone to work as a team. She probably read the phrase in an article about the importance of teamwork, but she did not encourage anyone to practice it.

The owner liked her anyway because she saved him money and he didn't care about his employees, he only cared, as so many owners of nursing homes do, about the bottom line and how much money he could rake in. The first year I was at St. Barley's they had a company Christmas party for the employees. We were given a written invitation from Madeline and the owner telling us we were invited to the party, which was to be held at a local restaurant. The invitation also had a notation at the bottom informing us we could not bring spouses or family to the party. I was so pissed by that notation that I planned to not go, if they were going to be so cheap. Crystal, the Social Services Director talked me into going though. She said: "Look, think of it as a free dinner and drinks on the boss. Think of it as a night out with the girls." I did go and everyone seemed to have a good time. The next year, Madeline decided everyone had been too rowdy and people had too good of a time. Some of the nurses had played drinking games and they were harmless enough, but Madeline didn't like it. At the first party no one sat with Madeline either, except for the Admissions/Marketing person who was always trying to suck up anyway. That second Christmas party now, according to that year's invitation, going to be held in the nursing home's main dining room. When I asked about the residents, Madeline said she was going to 'have the main dining room roped off to residents.' That pissed me off because now, instead of going away from work and being able to relax and have a good time, we would get to continue our work and attend this party sporadically, if at all, and no drinks. If I had thought the previous year's party had been cheap, this one topped that by a mile. It also pissed me off that Madeline was acting like the staff, in particular her, owned the nursing home to the degree of invading the residents' home and their space as well. The second year's party was crap and no one had a good time. The owner did invite department heads out for drinks, but I didn't care to go rub elbows with the 'elite' from work, thank you very much. Madeline and the owner explained that nursing assistants, dietary, and maintenance, anyone they didn't consider good enough, in their eyes, was not invited to have drinks, as they did at the restaurant the previous year. Pretty much, this new way of having a holiday party was to save the owner more money. The owner, no poor man by any means and a once a year party would not break him. The day of the party, the main dining room had been roped off, some residents wanted to go in but were turned away by staff, a fact that burned quite a few families, and rightly so. Neither the owner nor the administrator had glowing personalities and neither was liked very much by the employees. I dare say they were liked even less after that party.

Back in our office I tell Crystal that I had promised Mary I could set up a care plan meeting with staff and her and her family, to discuss why Mary is unhappy. "Good luck there," is Crystal's reply. "Why?" I ask her. "It seems like a simple request to me," I say. "Yes it is, and it is Mary's right to want one," Crystal says to me. "But the staff, especially the nurses, hate scheduled care plan meetings. Good luck with throwing one in their plans that's not on the schedule," she says with a smile. I knew what she meant. I had worked nursing homes enough to know that while about 80% of nursing home staff like their jobs and are there because it is their chosen profession, there exists another 20% who are there for the paycheck alone. This is 2006 and the economy isn't great, especially for jobs, so the 20% for the paychecks are there because the medical field is hiring full force and it represents job security to them. It's on the Internet and the news all the time. I remember a commercial saying: "The fact is, Baby Boomers are getting older and they will need medical services. Consider nursing, Occupational Therapy or   Physical Therapy as a good career field." While the elderly have always been a commodity to the medical profession, that age group has come to be seen as a virtual gold mine to people in the medical field, especially in a bad economy.

I go on to tell Crystal I am going to set up the care plan meeting, whether the nurses like it or not, because Mary is so unhappy about being here and we need to help her find a solution to her unhappiness, if possible. It's not like the nurses hate Social Services in nursing homes, it's just that everyone in nursing homes look at the Social Services department as some sort of necessary evil that the state and federal government requires. Traditional nursing homes are run on the Medical Model type set up and nurses see the rest of the staff, in nursing homes, as needed but we have no valid opinions, in the nurses' eyes since we aren't medical people. I would say nurses don't necessarily hate Social Services in nursing homes, but at St. Barley's, the

Director of Nursing (DON) made no bones about how much she disliked our department. She disliked it so much that, at times, she thought she was best suited to run Social Services, to her liking. It didn't seem to bother the DON that we were two separate professions and Social Services would not presume to try and run the nursing department. At St. Barley's, many of the staff thought Social Services was such a cake job that anyone off the street could do it just as effectively as those of us with a degree. In fact, I even hold a Master's Degree, but to the staff, especially the DON, that fact held no water. Their opinion was: "How hard can Social Services be?" Too many nursing homes, these days, do try to use nurse case managers to try and save a buck. But in my opinion, nursing is nursing and Social Work is social work. Apparently Social Work is hard enough that every state requires a degree to perform the duties well, is what I was tempted to tell them.

Even the LPN's thought we were there for window dressing and simply because the governments require we be there. I remember talking to a friend, who holds a BS as an RN, she once told me not to worry about their opinions. She even laughed and said: "Listen, to those of us RN's with a

BS, the term LPN stands for let's play nurse anyway." She tells me my 6 years of college outweighs their opinions about my profession. Easy for her to say, since she works in a hospital where the staff seem to respect Social Workers much more than at St. Barley's. She also laughed at our DON's credentials because our DON had been an LPN who got into the accelerated program designed to crank out RN's faster for the demanding market. My friend said she had much more training obtaining her four year degree than our own DON had. I knew all of this was true, but at St. Barley's it didn't seem to matter how well you did your job. All that mattered was how well anyone could kiss the Administrator's ass. In that area, the DON held a Master's. Hell, even our Admissions and Marketer, with no degree whatsoever, seemed to be in competition with the DON in the area of ass kissing. It was like they were trying to outdo each other and see who could brown nose the best. Apparently if you stroked the Administrator's ego, you were smarter than anyone else at St Barley's, at least in her eyes.

I did go to the DON and told her I promised Mary a care plan meeting. The DON rolled her eyes, audibly sighed and said we could have one, if we absolutely had to. I told her Mary needed to say what is on her mind to us and her family so we could work on a solution, of sorts. I also told her how Mary has taken to sitting in her room and is crying all of the time. I start back to our office and I see Mary in the front lobby sitting on the sofa. I figure this is a good time to stop and say hello to her. I ask her if I may sit down next to her, she says: "It's your place, do what you want." I no sooner sit down when I see a nurse frantically waving for me to come over to her. I excuse myself to Mary and go to where the nurse is standing. "Mary says she is waiting for a cab to take her home. Did you know that?" I tell her I did not know it since I had no more than said hello to Mary. "Well she is. You need to talk to her. Tell her she is not going anywhere." I look at the nurse and tell her we are not a prison and if Mary is bent on going home, I cannot stop her from doing so. "I don't see why not," the nurse says. I tell her I will see what is going on with Mary.

I go back to where Mary is sitting and ask her how things are going. She looks at me and says: "I'm calling a cab and I'm getting the hell out of here," she tells me. I ask her if something has happened since we last talked. "No, it's just that this damned place isn't my home, I told you that," she says. I nod and say I remember her telling me that. I also tell her I have set up a meeting, like we talked about. She looks at me and sighs, as if exasperated. I ask her if maybe she can hold off going home until after the meeting so I can set up home services she may need. "My granddaughter isn't going to listen anyway. My daughter used to look in on me every day but she died in a car accident last year," she explains to me. "My granddaughter just doesn't have the time for me. She wants to sell my house and take my money," she says, as her voice cracks. "Besides, if I am annoying enough, maybe I'll get kicked out of here then my granddaughter will have to take me home," Mary says. "First of all, St. Barley's will get all your money, so you don't have to worry about your granddaughter getting any of it," I want to tell her, but I refrain from saying so. I tell her the meeting will address her concerns and maybe we can set up services for her to return home eventually. She reluctantly agrees. While this conversation is going on, the Activity Director walks by. She has heard part of the conversation and approaches Mary. "Why don't you come to the activity going on right now?" she asks Mary. "What is it?" Mary asks her. "We are watching

Garfield the Movie in the lounge," the Director explains.

"That movie is for kids," Mary answers. "But it's happy and funny and upbeat," the Activity Director says in her most convincing voice. "No thanks," Mary says. "I'd rather sit in my room," Mary says as she walks down the hall. "I tried," the Activity Director says, shrugging her shoulders.

I understood why this activity didn't appeal to Mary. Most of the activities at St. Barley's are kid friendly, more so than for adults. Mostly the only ones who filter in to see this kind of movie are the residents with dementia. They only show up because an activity person has wheeled them into the lounge. This sort of activity also is easy for the Activity Department because they just have to load a movie into the player and no real activity is required on the staff's part. At a time in their life when people need to be more active, this is the sort of garbage that is offered at St. Barley's. All residents have to do is sit and watch, no range of motion required, no thinking either.

I get back to our office where I'm given a Behavior Sheet by one of the Nurse Aides. She tells me that Edward is refusing to allow staff to change his undergarment and he is soaking wet. She tells me she told him he cannot go to the dining room for coffee until it's changed. I look at her and ask her why another Aide cannot approach him to see if they can help him. "He is my person and I need to do it," she says to me. "Aren't we a team?" I ask her. "Maybe so, but he is mine and I have a schedule to keep and he's making me fall behind already," she wails. Yes, the proverbial schedule is more important than individuals, I think to myself. I go down the hall to talk to him and I am stopped by a man sitting near the doors going out into the garden area. "When in hell are they going to unlock the outside doors?" the gentleman asks me. I tell him I will find out and I go to the front desk to get the key. The front desk person tells me the temperature is too hot, so no one can go outside today. I say: "What did you say?" She repeats what she just told me. I explain to her these people are adults and should be able to decide on their own if they want to go outside. She glares at me and says it is St. Barley's policy that if temperatures are too cold or too hot, no one goes outside. I ask her if she will be going outside sometime today. She says she fails to see the correlation. I ask her if anyone is refusing to allow her access to the outside. "That's different," she tells me. I say I don't see how it is different. I leave, because I have to talk to Edward about being wet. I pass by the outside doors to the garden and see now there are several people waiting to go outside. I explain to them the policy and I hear one guy mutter: "Bull shit," as I start to leave. "My sentiments, exactly," I think to myself. I am always wondering why adults, who ran their own lives before coming to St. Barley's, now have a host of rules they have to abide by. I see more and more why Mary, and anyone else, hates living in a traditional nursing home.

I turn the corner and see Edward in the hall walking in the opposite direction so I catch up to him and ask him if one of the aides can assist him with changing his undergarment. He looks at me, smiles and says: "Sure, no one said they couldn't." I thank him for his cooperation and tell one of the aides they can assist him now. I go back down the hall wondering why the aide or even a nurse, couldn't just have handled the problem as well as I did.

I am stopped, once again, by everyone sitting by the doors going to the garden area; the group has gotten much larger now. I walk up to the desk and ask for the key to the outside door. The desk person starts to say something, but I shoot her a look that says she would do better to just not go there with me again. I hold out my hand and she gives me the key. "It's kind of hot out there today," the desk person says. "So send out aides with more glasses of water for people so they don't dehydrate and ask people if they want to stay outside or come in, after a while," I say to her. "I guess we could do that," she replies. I smile, take the keys and unlock the outside doors. The people who were waiting to go out rush the door and I assist several people in their wheel chairs outside. The smiles and look of utter delight on their faces is priceless indeed. I just cannot imagine anyone telling me I can or can't go outside. As one resident at St. Barley's said to me recently: " The American dream is more like the American nightmare times ten and in here, all of us old people are lumped together in people's minds, we are all the same in their eyes. It's like we were real people when we were younger, but now we live here, we have no personalities, and I guess we lost em once we walked through those big glass doors. Now we are hot house plants, we can't go out alone, or go down to the river alone, if anything happens to us, people here (staff) worry about their own asses, like someone is going to blame them if we died someplace other than our safe beds."

There is no reason, if a resident enjoys colder weather and some snow, why they cannot be allowed outside then either, with staff assistance. Residents own coats and scarves and gloves and mittens. They should be allowed to use the winter gear, to bundle up and go outside to see and experience the snow if they so wish. Nursing homes should have greenhouses too, even if they are only mini ones for residents to be able to grow some fresh herbs and vegetables to eat year round. No one should ever have restrictions about going outside and having access to the outdoors at anytime in their life.

There should be picnic tables and outdoor grills when people's families visit. Usually grills were only used if it was a 'special' occasion, again, when staff decided it was appropriate. Residents and staff should participate in grilling outside at least once a week in a nursing home. This would be a fun activity and would also be a good part of the staff/resident bonding process. I know some people are more sensitive to sunlight due to certain medications, but staff can be more diligent about extra precautions. Staff just need to be sure residents wear loose fitting clothes in hot weather so clothes do not stick to skin; be sure residents wear large hats for head and shade protection. Make sure residents don sunglasses and if someone does not own a pair, Activities should always have a selection to choose from for anyone to use. Outdoor gardens also offer a pleasant setting loved ones to sit and visit; they should include bird houses and pretty lighting fixtures. This not only offers a nice place to visit, but it encourages family and friends to come back often to visit loved ones.

Gardening tools can be modified by the therapy department, just as eating utensils can be modified, so that older people can easily grasp tools or reach the garden area from wheel chairs.

It is therapeutic for elderly to work tools, as best they can, and to keep fingers and limbs in working order and improve, or maintain their range of motion by encouraging the use of all motor skills.

For people suffering from depression, being outside in natural light, and feeling useful because they are contributing to garden maintenance, can be very therapeutic for their self-esteem and mood by taking in the wonderful sights, smells and sounds in a garden area. Gardening promotes relaxation and helps to ease stress levels which also help to reduce anxiety symptoms as well.

Gardening helps to promote social interaction with other residents and their families when a group gets together to plan and care for a garden. If the garden includes food plants, many residents will, sometimes more readily eat fresh produce they have helped to grow. Vegetable garden beds can be raised or trellises can be utilized to make it easier for elderly people to reach plants and to harvest the vegetables.

Growing and picking of vegetables can also lead to wonderful exchange of recipes among residents and the creation of some wonderful dishes for all to enjoy. Many elderly people, especially in rural areas, grew up on farms and many lived with spouses on farms. Elderly people have many wonderful recipes and good ideas about how to use fresh vegetables, and cooking also leads to social interaction, which improves well-being and maintains motor skills and range of motion.

Locking residents inside because of weather should never be an option. At St. Barley's it's as if people suddenly become two years old and need staff to tell them everything. I can think of no greater insult than to have a staff member grab my wheel chair and say: "No, you cannot go out the door." Whenever this happens, the staff person saying no almost always has a look of surprise on their face when a resident becomes resistant or even combative. Grabbing a person's wheel chair to either stop re-direct them from going someplace, or to move them out of the way for staff's convenience, is, in itself, rude. A wheel chair is an extension of the person and grabbing it is just like grabbing a person's arm and shoving them out of the way.

The Elderly Fear Nursing Homes; Not Surprised?

If you bring up the subject of a nursing home to most people, you will always get a strong reaction. Either people try to steer you off of the subject, because it makes them uncomfortable, or they say things like: "I'd rather be dead than have to spend my life in one of those places." Very seldom are people neutral when it comes to the feelings about a traditional nursing home, if asked for their opinions. The elderly, especially, are no exception.

In the fall of 2007, an independent company ran a survey asking elderly people what they feared most about growing older. The results were this; the majority of elderly

feared the prospect of having to live the rest of their lives

in a nursing home more than they feared death. The survey

stated that only 3% of seniors surveyed actually feared death.

To many elderly in our society, nursing homes are inhumane

places. Places where no one, in their right mind, wants

to live and they represent losing our dignity once we are

assigned to live in one. When an older person is assigned to

a nursing home, as one resident said: "It's social suicide and

we all know it. We are put in here because people, mostly

our people, want us out of sight and out of mind. We may be

old, Honey, but we aren't stupid, at least not all of us, yet."

I realize not many people in our society are concerned

with what happens to elderly people in nursing homes,

although, unless people plan to live forever, they will grow

old and should be very concerned.   Whatever anyone

feels about this subject, the fact is, we all will grow old, no

exceptions, excluding those who die young, and these issues,

concerning nursing homes; will eventually need to be faced

by nearly everyone but the very rich, in American society.

Recently many people have been quite upset over the

public health care debate because certain factions in the debate seem to be fixated on what some have dubbed 'death squads.' The death squad debate seems to stem from some people thinking it will be mandatory for physicians to have end of life discussions with elderly patients. If this is what some people consider death squads, then nursing homes in America have already been acting as such death squads, it is simply that no one noticed or cared, until we started to debate public health care. I have worked with the elderly, in different capacities, for many years, for a while as a home health aide, as a nursing assistant and most recently, as a Social Services Director. If Americans think President Obama has placed stipulations in his health care proposal about 'death squads' because they think it will be mandatory for older people to discuss end of life plans with their doctors, then nursing homes have always fit this description. Staff members in the nursing home, where I worked as a Social Services Director, were always approaching me to 'discuss end of life, or Hospice plans' with the elderly and their families. It seems nursing home staff eventually do get tired of sending elderly people to the ER when they become ill because 'the ER cannot do anything more for them anyway' as the reasoning goes. Unfortunately they are correct because Emergency Room personnel will only do so much and apparently feel time and life saving efforts are 'wasted' on very old, very frail people. The problem, when the elderly decide to get hospice services, is Medicare will not pay for any more room and board in a nursing home, so families have to pay out of pocket for their loved one to stay in the nursing home, which can be a significant cost. Sometimes when a person needs hospice, they have come in to a facility for therapy and Medicare is covering the cost, so the choice may now become; pay out of pocket for room and board or, if you have no money left, you get to die in pain so as not to lose your Medicare. As the laws are set up right now, Hospice workers are able to get a higher dose of medications to help ease any suffering the dying individual may experience as the body's mechanisms begin to shut down. A dying person usually will experience much anxiety because of this also. Hospice workers can obtain higher doses of anti-anxiety medications to help with this anxiety. No dying person should have to die in pain and needless suffering. We, as Social Workers, were discouraged from offering Hospice services to families, even when it was clear they were dying. The nursing home would place people on what they called comfort measures. Those measures were exactly that, to keep the person comfortable, something the nursing home does for everyone anyway. Unfortunately those measures are not enough to really help keep a person comfortable, but to simply mean they would not be sent to the ER needlessly. Comfort measures do, however, allow the nursing home to milk Medicare of payments by having the therapy departments write up bogus therapy orders so they can bill Medicare. It's a scheme of the worst kind simply to line the nursing home's pocket. And a good number of people cannot return home for hospice services either, because many residents either have no family left, or they have no one who can be in their homes with them 24 hours a day, which is required by hospice for home care. The nursing home directors try to discourage hospice care because it can mean the facility gets no more Medicare payments, which means it guarantees the facility gets their money, where paying out of pocket does not. Medicaid recipients, whose family request hospice services, are covered for up to 95% of their room and board; however, if a resident does not qualify for Medicaid the room and board must be paid out of pocket.

It is not unusual for a hospital to be in such a hurry to discharge an elderly patient; they come to a nursing home in need of hospice care. This certainly does not sound like any choice I would care to have to make when I am ill. Worse yet, I would hate to burden my loved ones with making those difficult choices for me either.

After talking to people over the years who had come to a nursing home, either to live or just for a short stay to complete therapy to be able to return home, it seems almost unanimous among them that what they all fear most about having to live in a nursing home is; loss of independence, loss of autonomy of being able to go where they want to go whenever they want to, fear of being forgotten, fear of being able to make their own decisions and fear of no longer being a part of a community. Basically, they fear losing all of the things we take for granted that help contribute to everyone's quality of life. Especially the ability to make their own choices in daily living, such as; shopping when and where we want to, when we want to go to bed, when we want to get up, when we want to decide to take our medications, if we want to have a cocktail and even something as simple as deciding if we want to go outside or not, no matter what the season is. Once a person loses their independence they often lose their will to live. Sometimes, if the elderly think it is expected of them to be less independent, they may walk slower, they may lose their cognitive abilities more rapidly and all of this can be detrimental to their health as well. Loss of independence can make an elderly person feel isolated and often leads to depression.

In the case of Mary, mentioned earlier; we have the care plan meeting with her and her family. Her family consists of her oldest son, her granddaughter and her granddaughter's husband. The nurse assigned to Mary, the physical therapy person, the dietitian and Social Services, me, are also present. I do notice that Mary's nurse aide is not present, when I ask about this I am told it is not policy to ask the aides to attend. I know that nurse aides are the primary care givers and probably know more about Mary than any nurse who only dispenses her medications to her. The nurse aides care for her and assist her daily, yet in traditional nursing homes, are left out of the all important care plan meetings. There is a critical shortage of nursing assistants in America, and I can see why this is when I notice how they are treated in traditional nursing homes.

Anyway, back to Mary's meeting. A month later, since Mary came to St. Barley's for rehab, she had taken to staying in her room all day, except to come to the lobby to call a cab, and she quit eating. By the time Mary's meeting takes place, she looks haggard, skinnier and has bags under her eyes like she hasn't been sleeping much. I visited her nearly every day and had voiced concerns to the nurse. The nurse's response was to ask the MD for sleep medication and an anti-depressant. None of those medications had seemed to help Mary much. The physical therapy person starts out by explaining why it is unsafe, in her opinion, for Mary to live by herself in her own home. To the therapist, the MD and Mary's family, it makes perfect sense for Mary to live at St. Barley's where she will be better taken care of, in their eyes. Mary responds by telling them it is easy for them to say because it is her life, not theirs, that is being disrupted. After a meeting that takes an hour and a half, her granddaughter and son agree to allow Mary to return home in three weeks and they will take turns, along with a neighbor, to look in on Mary to be sure she is safe. They agree only if Mary will allow the link to life services, which involves wearing a necklace with a button to push for help, if she falls or becomes ill. Mary, with tears in her eyes, agrees to this. It is settled, she will go home in a few short weeks.

This turned out to be a good solution to Mary's problems and her unhappiness about living in a nursing home. What about those residents who either have no family, or the family lives a long way away? All a traditional nursing home can offer in those cases is usually medications; medications for sleep, for appetite or medications for depression. I never heard, in traditional nursing homes, that the solution should be to usher in culture changes of any kind. The facilities always feel the resident has the responsibility to conform to the facility, not the other way around. Whenever St Barley's administrator mentioned culture change, it was nothing to really make the residents' lives nicer, or richer. To her, it was simply for marketing purposes only, to give the illusion of a significant change. Traditional nursing homes are always facility oriented, not person oriented, yet they make it their business to deal with people.

Down the hall in a different wing at St. Barleys, another new resident, Carol recently told me how she 'put herself in here because she did not want her family to have to worry about checking up on her all the time.' But she does say, with some bitterness in her tone: "I have six god dam children and not one of em can seem to take me in, the damned ingrates." Carol is in relatively decent health, but she is legally blind due to macular degeneration and cannot drive and finds it difficult to live on her own anymore. Even further down the hall, in another wing, a married couple, Mr. and Mrs. Doran reside. Mr. Doran, much like Mary, has taken to crying, on occasion, and tells how he and his wife have spent the entire $100,000 they had 'saved for retirement' to pay for their stay here. He says now that the cash has been spent, they have to put their house of 40 years up for sale to continue to live here. He says he wishes they had spent every cent on enjoying an early retirement, but, instead it has all gone for room and board and medications due to his wife's sudden illness. The sad look in the husband's eyes tells me the optimism he once felt about retirement has been replaced by hopelessness and despair. Both of them are now in their 70's and he is not strong enough to do the lifting that is required in order to take care of his wife's needs in their home. All of these people, even though they reside in the same nursing home, are each experiencing different attitudes about the whole experience. One resident appears somewhat satisfied she made the 'right' decision to live in the nursing home, but the decision was based on what she felt her family needed and has expressed that she would prefer to be living 'in her own home', and the second one is feeling like he and his wife have been cheated out of a pleasant retirement and now they help support an impersonal nursing home with their hard earned money. This sort of drama unfolds way too often in nursing homes all across America. I have witnessed the despair felt by some people who find that they are living in a nursing home suddenly and who not only hadn't made plans to live in one, but somehow thought it would never happen to them. Yet there they were, living not exactly what they thought their 'golden years' would be like at all.

Why Did I Work With the Elderly?

I guess you may be wondering how I came to work with the elderly in nursing homes or even why I got into Social Work. The traditional nursing homes in America are, by far, a major problem. If the facilities in America changed from the medical model type of set up to a more person centered style, most of the usual problems that seem to be presented by the elderly in those places would start to subside. If nursing homes all changed over to culture change, then they would, at least, be pleasant places to live because no one wants to live in a hospital. A hospital is exactly what traditional nursing homes resemble. The institutions, as they are right now, cause most of the problem behaviors the elderly may be experiencing.

In 1987 I got divorced from a very bad marriage and moved out on my own. After years of nowhere, dead end jobs, I decided to go to college at the age of 42. I had two young boys to support and a college degree seemed to be the sensible route for me. After my divorce I had needed help for a while and I applied for services for the boys and myself. I noticed some of the social workers were kind and compassionate, while others seemed harsh and judgmental. I liked helping people so social work seemed, to me, to be the best way to help.

I had been a nursing assistant, working for nursing homes as well as a home health aide, for many years. I did not like, as an aide, how we were treated and I liked the crummy pay even less. I did, however, love working with the elderly residents and, for the most part, they all were very sweet.

While attending college, most of the social work majors talked about working with kids because they seem to have more of a bright future, or working with families, but for the kids' sakes. I never once heard a social work major say they wanted to work with the elderly and never in a nursing home.

Once I graduated I did start out being a coordinator for a juvenile program, working with at-risk youth, ages five up to the age of about eleven. I liked the job, but it was a non-profit and there was talk of the program probably being cut because the funding was running out. I then went to work as an outreach case manager working with MR/DD and those adults suffering from mental illnesses. Some of the adults with mental illnesses could get irate and sometimes violent. I was never attacked personally, but some of the case managers told stories of having been. Some of the adult males had recently been released from prison and it could be kind of scary at times. Part of my job was transporting the clients in the company van to various appointments, including appointments to see our agency psychiatrist. Sometimes they could get pretty belligerent and, at times, I envisioned someone having to look for my dead body in one of the area cornfields since it was a small, rural community.

I applied for Social Services Assistant when I saw the ad for St. Barleys went to the interview and within the week was hired. I loved working with the elderly as a social worker even more than as a nursing assistant because I felt I had more power to help them.

After six months of working at St. Barley's, the Social Services Director told me she had gone to an interview at the local college. She applied for that job after, Madeline, the administrator, had given Crystal her yearly evaluation. Madeline had told Crystal she 'was not a team player' which upset Crystal a lot. Crystal, being convinced that Madeline hated her, began looking for another job. Between the Administrator being harsh and always holding the club of 'you will be fired for nothing' over her head and the DON being a total bitch and trying to run the Social Services Department, it just proved too much for Crystal to take anymore. I did not blame her, no one should have to swallow Prozac daily, like she was, just to be able to report to work and function amid overbearing stress.

Crystal was soon hired by the college and put in her resignation. Her resignation began a series of interviews for the position of Social Services Director. I put my name in for the position, but Madeline felt that because I had a master's degree, I might want too much money and refused to even consider me for the position. Madeline felt she could get someone fresh out of college much cheaper than what she had been paying Crystal. Many people applied, some with experience, but mostly not. Madeline decided on one young girl, fresh out of college, who had a degree in women's studies. This was fine with Madeline since she always felt anyone could do social work, even if they had no experience with the elderly. This young girl turned out to be perky and her personality ended up being too perky for Madeline. The young girl also had no idea what she was doing, as far as the paperwork was concerned either, so she soon, within six weeks time, became frustrated anyway and sent Madeline an email saying she had resigned.

A few days later, Madeline decided to pull another resume from her files and another woman was picked. The problem with this one was the day she was to show up for orientation; she called and said she had changed her mind. Madeline again pulled one of the resumes and hired one more woman. This woman lasted, again, about six weeks and Madeline decided to let her go. This last woman could not remember to make it to morning meetings. Every day she was either late or had just forgotten to show up altogether. Finally, after all of this, Madeline decided to offer me the position. By this time I wasn't even sure if I wanted the damn position anymore, but Madeline did offer me more money so I decided to take it after all. Long before we started the hiring blitz, I had been doing the job, by myself, for about six weeks before Madeline had even decided to hire the first person on her list.

What also made being alone even more fun was the fact it was spring and this was the time the state surveyors were due to come in and check our books and inspect how the place was being run. Surveyors are a ragtag lot because they never look for the same thing in every facility and never give a damn either about if the facility resembles anyone's home. They look for dust over a door jam, if anyone got psych services was the paperwork correct? Were the residents getting their meals with the correct number of hours in between each one? Most of what they look for is stupid and institutional-oriented anyway. Just before the state shows up, there is a frenzy of making sure things are 'done right' and data is up to date in charts and most of the entire sacred state book where surveyors look for updated data from each department. Most of this crap is never worried about the rest of the year, but now, due to inspections coming up, it makes employees run around like chickens with their heads cut off.

I ended up coming in at six in the morning and working until five or six every evening from a week until the surveyors show up until they are done with the inspections, which was two weeks later due to the fact this year they are two people short, two who either retired or quit. Not one time do the surveyors care if anyone has a private room, or a place to make tea, coffee or snacks, it is inspected like the institution that it is run as.

That, in a nut shell is how I took on the position of Social Services Director, one of the most thankless positions there. Director of a department that is merely tolerated and is expected, for the most part, to be a messenger or an extension of the Administrator and nursing and to do their dirty work for them so they don't need to look bad.

I did this job for about two years, when, one day, Madeline decided I wasn't a 'team player' because I stuck up way too much for the residents' rights, which I saw as my job. Before you quickly decide this book is written because I am a disgruntled former employee, I really feel no animosity toward St. Barley's. What I have done, however, is put things in perspective concerning traditional nursing homes. It is not unusual for traditional nursing homes go through social workers like crazy because most all of the traditional facilities end up making them choose, sooner or later, between what's good for the residents and what the company wants. St. Barley's was no exception to this trend. Madeline and the owner always tried playing the let's see how much we can get away with when it came to residents' rights. So one day Madeline called me into her office and said she had to 'let me go.' Besides I was now 59 years old and neither Madeline nor the DON really liked older people much and with that sort of attitude, a nursing home is always a good place to be working. The Administrator rarely came out of her office so if you were summoned to her office, it was via email or she would buzz you on the phone. This woman is grossly overweight, so it felt like I was going to see

Jabba the Hutt in the Creature Cantina every time I was summoned.

She had hired me an assistant a few months earlier. A young guy, fresh out of college with no experience working with the elderly either. I had to teach him everything from scratch because his only experience was in construction work fresh out of college.

I recently read an article on the Internet that listed the 'top ten jobs with high stress and low pay.' I was not surprised to find Social Work as number one on that list. I was thinking that Social Work is stressful out in the world and you can take that stress and multiply it times 100 when working a traditional nursing home. Couple that stress in a nursing home with administrators, owners and/ or corporations that refuse to listen or give Social Work the respect they duly deserve, and it can become almost unbearable. It is unusual for a Social Worker to last more than a couple of years in traditional nursing homes. Most leave because they, many times are given the added jobs of marketing and admissions, leaving precious little time to actually do Social Work tasks, much less spend quality time with residents, when needed. Culture change would change all of that. Culture change, when practiced as it should be, would give Social Workers back the respect they deserve. It would give them back the time needed to spend with residents and they would not be expected to cover 120 residents, plus admissions plus marketing, on their own anymore. Unfortunately, as it stands now, good Social Workers go out the door like smoke at a time they are needed the most by a facility. It's high time nursing homes wake up and smell the culture change because culture change's time has come. It is very clear the nursing home system, as it is now, is broken and in dire need of a fix.

The Assistant

Finally, after weeks and weeks of not having much help and doing all of the Social Work by myself for over 100 residents, the Administrator hired an assistant for my department. He was very young and had worked in mostly the construction field since college. When he started as my assistant, all this kid knew about the elderly he had learned from a book. He was, however, a walking encyclopedia of stereotypes and myths, concerning the elderly population. Don't get me wrong, I don't hold youth against anyone, but most people do not fit into a tidy little book, there are simply too many variables. This guy had never, in his life worked with the elderly and it showed, but I was hoping he was going to be smart enough to absorb quickly what he was to be taught.

It turned out he was smart enough to pull the wool over the eyes of the mostly all female staff, except me. He was as charming as he was lazy, and boy was he ever lazy, with a capital L. I have always disliked the fact that nursing home workers are predominately female, because it has been my experience that when staff is predominately female, it is one big house of hormones and a perpetual bitch fest at times.

The DON of St. Barley's, at 35 realizing she was not getting any younger, fancied herself to be God's gift to everyone, but especially males of any age. The new Social Services Assistant would blow smoke up her ass and she would lap it up, and I must say the Administrator was nearly as gullible too. I knew the DON thought too highly of her own feminine appeal by the way she reacted whenever we changed any ancillary services offered to residents, particularly if the service was headed by a cute male. If we switched, say from a male podiatrist to a female one, she immediately would find fault with the female. This was very true of our psych services too. The best most nursing homes are going to get to visit for psych services is a psychologist. There is never enough money to make it worth a psychiatrist's time to visit old people. Anyway when I first started at St. Barley's, we had a male psychologist from an

❈

agency, who thought as equally as highly of himself as our DON did, so they got along famously. The Administrator, one day, decided she did not like the agency we were using for psych services and she changed services. The second agency also had a male psychologist, but this guy was a bit overweight and married, so the DON did not like him and bitched about every report he wrote, even though his reports proved to be more thorough than the previous psychologist's had been. This new, overweight, married one also did not flatter her and take her to a free lunch each time he visited, as the former one had apparently done for a long time. Even though it was the Administrator who did not like the old service and actually hired the new one, it did not matter in the least to the DON. In the DON's eyes it was Social Services who had influenced the hiring of the new agency so our department got all of the complaints from her about it.

So because of the lack of males at St. Barley's who deemed worthy of any flirting, the DON was definitely ripe for the Social Service Assistant's compliments, even though they were as false as a three dollar bill, but he knew how to manipulate most women. It did not work on me, so he did not waste his time and since he was a little snake and wanted my job anyway, he did not bother with the false bull shit on me. But, instead, I got to listen to his bitching behind the DON's back about how he really could not stand her, ditto for the Administrator as well.

He had told me his parents had divorced when he was very young and his mom left him and his sisters with his dad to raise four kids by himself. He knew that he was the darling of his family, being the youngest and only boy, and he admitted he really resented his mom for leaving. He said he hated his stepmother, so this, coupled with the mom resentment, made him pretty much a woman hater, or at the very least, a big user of women. He made it pretty plain he did not respect most women anyway because he felt they were too emotional and he hated working with them. This new assistant was so lazy that the very first week on the job he claimed his grandmother was on her death bed and he may need time off.

Low and behold, four days after he started working, his grandmother supposedly died. He immediately took a week off to help his mother with the funeral preparations, so he claimed. He actually turned out to be a constant and perpetual liar and a total disaster as a social work assistant.

Once that was out of the way, he returned to work, and I say work very loosely because he did everything but work. Most of the time, when he was not trying to talk on his cell phone instead of working, he would claim he was going to one of the units to chart, or to interview a resident, but after a couple of hours, I'd go to check on his progress and he would actually be chatting and flirting with the nurses instead of charting. He also, right from the start, took to calling himself, in phone conversations, the 'Assistant Director of Social Services', and came in everyday only about 10 or 15 minutes before morning meeting was to start. Many days he would oversleep and come in late or claim he had been caught in traffic, and the Administrator never once reprimanded him for oversleeping. He was so good at blowing smoke up the right people's ass; I began to think he'd missed his true calling as an actor because he could have won an academy award for his performances.

After only a month on the job as my helper, he started to whine about how he was not being paid enough for his services as the assistant. I suppose he felt that his making the women perceive they were wonderful, sucking up and not actually doing his job, made him a valuable asset to St. Barley's, so he felt underpaid. He started to look for what he called 'a job more worthy of his expertise', namely becoming an administrator in some other facility for the elderly, never mind he never got his present job duties down pat. He started to go to job interviews to be a director or administrator because he was a semi decent looking 26 year old male with no experience or background in working with elderly and decided he had become an expert in the field. But hell, he had been bullshitting his way through one month of working in a nursing home, so why not bullshit his way to the top.

I remember him telling me about one particular

job interview he went on for a position as Social Services Director in another nursing home. He was interviewed by a male administrator and it apparently was not so easy to fool another guy, the charm just did not work on him. He even told me: "I was interviewed by a guy so I knew I might not get the job. Female administrators are so much easier to manipulate." It turned out he was absolutely right, at least from his experiences at St. Barley's, anyway.

He got so good at sucking up that soon the Administrator was calling me in her office often to chew me out for things he did or did not do, until, eventually she 'let me go' because she said she 'expected more' from her Social Services Director. Come to find out, this little snake in the grass was telling the DON, who of course would tell the Administrator, he was 'looking for another job, because he wanted to be the Social Services Director. The DON, who loved the attentions of men, decided he was a bigger asset to the place, experience or not, so I had to go anyway in her mind. He of course, got the job when I was let go. I found out, through the grapevine that he lasted only about 8 months at St. Barley's after I left. I also found out that after he went to another facility to work it was discovered by the St Barley's Administrator that he had not charted like he was supposed to and did not keep his end of the work up. I suppose he wanted to get the hell out of St. Barley's before the state surveyors came in that year to find out how bad his work really was. Gee, there was a big shocker. I am not sure his wanting me to be let go stemmed from dislike of me or just fear and self-preservation, not to mention more money, until he could get another job before anyone else found out about him not really doing his job properly, especially since he couldn't work his charm on me and I had been making him correct his many mistakes.

If he had spent as much time actually doing his job as he had spent blowing false compliments up everyone's asses or talking on his cell phone or playing on the Internet on company time, trying to avoid work, he might have earned at least an ounce of respect from me.

I recently read an article on the Internet that said employment agencies in some areas were recommending that employers steer clear of the twenty-something workers because, as the article said, that age group tends to be lazy and unfocused. The article went on to explain many in that age group were more likely to be texting and bringing up their social network programs more often at work on the employer's time. I discovered first hand that this is quite true.

I even recall, in another supervisory position I held, a few years earlier, that my twenty-something assistant would try to spend her work hours calling caterers and flower shops and tried to plan her whole wedding on company time. I can't tell you how many times I reprimanded her for this and she would look at me like I had two heads or something. The work ethic in this age group is either very bad or nonexistent altogether.

The Age Appropriate Activities

State inspectors like to use the term 'age appropriate activities' when they check over what is being offered in nursing homes as formal activities when conducting their surveys. What in hell is an 'age appropriate activity' anyway? What business is it of surveyors if I collect, or even play with stuffed animals or dolls? Who in hell are they to come in and run my life for me by telling me what is age appropriate? The age appropriate label somehow hints that my behavior is now some sort of deviance because I may enjoy coloring in coloring books in my spare time, or using building blocks because I was an engineer or architect before coming to the facility. Like comfort foods and favorite clothing, maybe I derive comfort from using or wearing certain items and what business is it of surveyors to come in and tell me it may not be appropriate? This label is just another one of the little indignities and insults that people are bombarded with when they enter nursing homes.

I am guessing that by growing old and entering a facility, it is a popular opinion that my IQ has suddenly dropped a hundred or so points because I am older. What an insult this is to elderly people. Dementia may rob me of some faculties but if I do not have flaming dementia, leave me alone and let me live my damn life as I please, as long as it does not hurt anyone else.

On the subject of activities in nursing homes, I could just about write volumes about the crummy activities offered to older citizens in these places. Most 'activities' are a misnomer because a great deal of 'activities' do not involve being 'active' at all. There are way too many passive activities going on in nursing homes at a time in people's lives when they need to be active the most. Being active certainly helps to maintain a person's physical condition, their well being and helps maintain a healthy lifestyle. It is a big problem sometimes in faculties when few people want to attend activities. One big reason for this is because residents are asked on an intake sheet what activities they enjoy, but as a group, I have seen few of the activities offered to large groups. This may sound like a plug for the Nintendo Wii, but this game system is a wonderful boon for senior centers and nursing homes. It is a mildly passive activity but it helps to maintain people's range of motion, even if a person has a limited range of motion. Nursing homes cannot offer bowling alleys or golf courses, but the Nintendo Wii offers virtual ones. Many residents were used to bowling and golfing before entering the facility and this wonderful system offers those activities to them again. Activities that many people thought were closed to them once they entered the facility. Many facilities offer entertainment such as people playing instruments or boring sing-a-longs, but like candy or desserts, these should not be offered on a regular day to day basis in a diet that should be active-rich. The facility where I worked only offered trips to the local bar for lunches occasionally and, like I said, most activities did not involve being active at all, except for physical therapy, and physical therapy was offered only if the facility could milk Medicare benefits. The 'activities' were mostly watching stupid movies such as children's cartoon movies. There were no quilting bees, no making Christmas ornaments, no baking cookies, breads or anything, no knitting or crocheting bees and bingo was offered weekly but bingo is not a very active exercise and not everyone likes bingo either. Also offered were current events or travel log and the above mentioned activity of the local bar for lunch was only for those who could participate, meaning only for those residents who could easily be taken across the street. I recall one lady who wanted to go so badly but activities wouldn't take her because her wheel chair was more difficult to maneuver. This lady would ask me weekly why she didn't get to go and I would, in turn, ask the activity department the same thing, with no real answers, even when I offered to help wheel her myself. If it was particularly difficult to wheel a resident over across the street, that resident wasn't invited. There should also have been visits from residents living in other nursing homes with lunches provided for such visits or even the visiting residents bringing a bag lunch.   None of this was offered and hardly anyone moved around at all during most activities offered at St. Barley's.

St. Barley's was a typical nursing home where there is too few staff for too many residents so consequently, residents become bored, and this can create behaviors as well as depression. All human beings need social stimulation, even residents with dementia and Alzheimer's.   The Activity Department should also have been holding as many activities outside as possible. Maybe a resident is proficient in gardening tips and some residents may be interested in a talk from them about houseplants and how to care for some plants. There should be discussions about the latest book, like a book club meeting, even residents who cannot see to read can get talking books if they wish to participate. Residents could offer up favorite recipes for the kitchen staff to cook for them and other residents in the facility. The residents who love to cook could conduct a fun cooking class for any resident who wants to learn how to make certain dishes. This would be a wonderful opportunity for residents from various ethnic backgrounds to share their ethnic heritages through favorite dishes. Residents could participate in crocheting and knitting sessions and maybe even offer lessons to young people in the community who might like to learn to knit or crochet. These lessons could be offered to anyone who cares to learn how. There should be a computer room in facilities, those who do not know how to use a computer could be offered computer classes. Exercise sessions should be offered outside, if people were outside more often, perhaps less sleep medications and less anti-depressants would be needed for residents because we all know how beneficial fresh air and sunlight are to promote well being and health in anyone. Perhaps the nursing homes could advertise to the community to offer free gardening sessions and free tips to the community concerning gardening. Everyone loves to feel useful and needed and how wonderful for residents to share knowledge with the community. Maybe residents could all work on compiling a book about gardening or a cook book of favorite recipes to sell within the community.

Residents could also offer free knitting or crocheting lessons to anyone who would be interested in learning. This is a wonderful way for mothers and daughters to spend quality time with each other, with residents, as well as offering outside interactions with the community for residents. There could be weekly card lessons for young people, or anyone, wanting to learn how to play Euchre or Pinochle. In this electronic age, many of those quieter games have been almost forgotten. There are so many ways nursing homes can interact with the immediate community and, in turn, the community can get to know residents in the facility and see how people live within the facility. Musicals in the afternoon on the nursing home lawn would be nice; this would enable residents to enjoy lawn concerts in summer, just like people living in the community enjoy them.

Residents love to get out and about and I am sure residents would love to attend high school and even college sports events. I am sure the students would also love to have extra fans rooting for them, sitting in the audience.

Picnics in a nearby park, for those who can get out would be lovely also, and for those who cannot get to those, there could be picnics held at the facilities which could include all the games we love to play at family reunions. A good game of horseshoes was always my father's favorite and think of the range of motion exercises it offers for stiff arms. With the new fire rings offered for outdoor activities anymore, I am sure residents would love marshmallow and weenie roasts and even swap camping stories, sitting around a 'campfire' and reminiscing.

Nursing homes could even stage their own carnivals, have trips to the county fairs and even have their own small community fairs on the grounds of the nursing home itself. I even think it would be fun for Administrators to sit in a dunking booth and let residents toss balls at the target to dunk them. I sure knew of several employees who would gladly fill the money boxes and line up to pay for a chance at dunking the Administrator.

Life and activities does not have to be boring at a nursing home. The Baby Boom generation could watch the Rocky Horror Picture Show at Halloween time and be encouraged to 'dress up' as their favorite character in the movies, as many did so years ago when it first came out. There could even be a midnight showing of the movie like there were years ago when it first made its debut. Residents could interact by waving light sticks as audiences who used to wave candles and lighters during some scenes did. I am sure male residents would enjoy watching old WWII movies with Audie Murphy, and everyone loves classic musicals from the old days. If the nursing home does not have a host of movies in stock, the Activity Director can borrow them from the local library. In fact, I am sure many residents would enjoy a trip to the library to pick out free movies.

The point is, not everyone likes bingo and bingo is usually just convenient for nursing home staff. It is easy to run, but sometimes activity staff wants to assist people to place the right chip on the right number and maybe not every resident cares enough to have it 'right.' I know budgets are tight, but most of the prizes given out at nursing home bingo are not anything I would particularly like very much at all. Most are dollar store trinkets or junk that has been donated, basically, something no one really wants anyway. So say goodbye to bingo in the facility because this is a new age of elderly coming onto the scene.

*

The facility where I worked offered bake sales so the Activity Department could earn money for the residents to have more activities. The problem with this was employees were expected to bake items at home and donate them. The residents would have probably enjoyed actually baking items and selling them. The Activity Director did not even invite residents to man the tables in order to sell the baked goods either. That Activity Department took away what few decisions residents were left to make on their own.

Where Are the pets?

Another aspect of most traditional nursing homes is the lack of the presence of animals. Many residents are used to owning a cat or a dog in their former lives on the outside. Every nursing home should have at least one cat and one dog; preferably more, so all residents could have access to them. It is a known medical fact that petting and loving an animal lowers people's stress levels and can even lower blood pressure. Let's face it; pets can have a very therapeutic affect for many people. The facility where I worked had a resident who used to own a cat at her home. Since there were no cats on the premises, she missed hers so badly that she carried a stuffed cat on her lap all day. The loss of her cat was probably one of the most devastating experiences this woman had to face. Her main concern was the fact that she had to give her cat away when she came to live in the facility.   Needless to say, my department had to care plan the fact she carried a stuffed cat because it was not 'age appropriate' behavior. If the facility had a cat that lived in the nursing home, I dare say the poor woman would not feel the need to carry a stuffed cat. We all know a stuffed cat or dog just are not the same. Cats and dogs offer affection to everyone in ways that a stuffed version just cannot cut it.   Many residents grew up on farms and some were running farms until they became frail and in need of a nursing home. Animals would be a great asset and influence on many residents' lives. The nursing home I worked in had a bird aviary where residents could passively sit and observe birds but they could not offer the therapeutic benefits of animals a person could pet or cuddle with. If residents want to bird watch, a facility should offer a van and rides to the meadows of the countryside or even city rooftops for bird watching. Even a tank of fish for residents to feed and watch would be a nice touch in every nursing home. I recall one day the activity department did arrange for a local farm to bring in a pig, a calf and a sheep and horse for residents to see. I will never forget the look of happiness on the residents' faces as they were petting and just plain watching the live farm animals.

Every week the residents of the nursing home where I worked would line the hallways and wait in eager anticipation for the pet visits to begin. Even those residents, who would seldom come out of their rooms for any other activity, would usually be excited and venture out to be able to play with the dogs when they visited. For many dementia residents an animal visit can often spark a memory and this will spur a topic of conversation that some residents seldom would have otherwise. Incorporating animals into the activities of the lives of residents is nice, but think of how much more enriched their lives would be if every facility had animals living there all the time. A bird aviary is nice, but there is something so rewarding about having a pet, or pets that residents could hold, cuddle as well as pet daily.

I think the pet visits offer residents a pure sort of love and acceptance they seldom feel in their daily lives in a facility. Residents have to put up with seeing the same faces daily and some residents get no family visitors or get few visits from family. The weekly pet visits are something they can count on weekly and they show excitement seldom seen in some residents otherwise. Imagine if facilities had their own pets that lived within the facility and residents could see and play with them daily. This sort of involvement with animals would, in many cases, be more beneficial than any therapy program the nursing home has to offer.

Pets in a nursing home can conjure up memories of childhood pets and these memories can be very therapeutic for many residents. Residents who may be self-absorbed will usually get caught up in thinking of the pet and not so much about their own, personal problems which is beneficial for people to have something else to think about other than pain.

Some nursing homes have dog obedience classes on the premises and this can be very entertaining and stimulating for residents to watch. Obedience classes also bring people from the community into the facility and any interactions with the general population for residents are very beneficial because residents feel they have more contact with the outside world. More contact with the community can benefit the community as well because having more visitors shows the community that a good nursing home is not something to be feared.

I am sure that having pets in a nursing home attracts animal lovers among the staff members and those who care for animals usually are compassionate to people as well. I am also sure that having pets in a facility would go a long way with helping staff retention by making it a wonderful place to work every day.

Facilities could be working with a local animal shelter to find 'just the right pets' and is a wonderful idea for both residents and the animals because residents and animals alike would definitely benefit from all the added attention.

Residents could interact with the outside community by inviting pet owners to come to the facility and have a dog show. Residents could make up awards and even participate in voting for their favorite animal in different categories.

Animals can help reduce loneliness, grief, fear and pain. St. Barley's had a couple who lived there together for over ten years. After the wife died he started to regress and came out of his room less and less to intermingle. But I did notice that one of the few times he would come out and even have a faint smile on his face was when the animal visits took place.

Residents will sometimes freely open up around animals because animals provide a safe avenue for communication. Animals do not judge us, do not talk back and are wonderful listeners and basically accept us for who we are. Animals don't care what kind of personal issues a person has, the animals live in the here and now. People will usually tell animals things they have never told any human being. Taking care of an animal also takes a person's mind off of their own problems, even if it is for a short while. A person caring for an animal must concentrate on caring for another living thing and attend to the animal's immediate needs and, in turn, this can make a person feel needed, which raises self-esteem. This helps people put focus onto something outside their own immediate problems and give them a better perspective and help increase a person's will to live.

Sometimes Administrators take a dim view of incorporating animals into the nursing home setting. Some fear other residents will have allergies or others will trip over animals and get hurt. They also fear residents will incur scratches or bites, but this is ridiculous because many elderly have animals in their private homes, some have several and for god reasons. Animals help alleviate any loneliness the elderly may start to experience as they age.

Animals make a place feel more like a home and much less like an institution and animals can help generate discussions whenever the elderly get together to chat. Animal antics will usually always make residents laugh, or at least smile while watching them, this hold true for even the most cantankerous resident.

This doesn't mean every family that tours a facility will like the idea of having animals living in the nursing home. That's fine, and if it's the case then maybe they are just too much into the idea of a facility as an institution or hospital. But if every nursing home, or at least many more of them, adopted animals as part of the permanent setting, most families would just take for granted that the animals are an integral part of the nursing home setting. A nursing home that attracts animal lovers as staff is wonderful too because I tend to feel more at home with people who love animals. Those who love animals are more likely, in my experience, to also give loving care to people too.

To help alleviate any burden placed on staff to

care for animals, a facility could employ a high
school or college student to come in each day to
feed, water, empty litter boxes and maybe even
transport an ailing animal to the local vet's office.
Maybe even volunteer groups would be able to
just volunteer for this service as well.

Abuse Takes Many Forms

Elderly are often scared of nursing homes because of the horror stories which tend to come out of nursing homes concerning resident abuse. Residents know their families cannot be with them in a facility 24 hours a day and many fear being ignored, or brushed off and not listened to because they may be considered senile. In fact, Science Daily (July 01, 2009), stated: "Complaints by the elderly are often treated as trivial by nursing home staff, which, in turn, makes it difficult for the elderly to influence their everyday lives." Most of all, older people are afraid of the fact that their complaints could rain retaliation down on their heads. Who is to say if the staff person who has been complained about will now be a little rougher in their care, or take longer when answering a call light, or even worse, out and out uncivilized to the person who complained? If the allegations are covered up well by other workers, which is quite likely in these situations, they will probably be considered unfounded by investigators, so the chances of the accuser having to deal with the person they had complained about, is very high indeed. This can make it quite bumpy for the person who had problems with this specific staff person to begin with, so imagine if you will how much more so now if the worker is still employed and caring for that resident who complained. There seems to be two major populations of people who are seldom listened to in our society, the very young and the very old.

While working in nursing homes, I have seen allegations of abuse covered up, verbal abuse especially, because it leaves no physical marks and it is a 'he said, she said' proposition, making it easier to conceal. I have seen residents' complaints brushed off because the complaining resident has been pegged as a chronic complainer, or simply as having misunderstood what was said. The fears elderly people in nursing homes have in this area are not without merit, and most times, very correct. The allegations of abuse may not be what we are familiar with such as hitting or name calling or even isolating anyone to their rooms. I have been appalled by what I called the small, daily assaults that can make a person's life miserable. On one occasion an incident I observed involved certain staff members who would make a habit of snapping at specific residents for various reasons during the course of the day. For instance, many staff members, including nurses, always had their 'favorites' and would treat them with more courtesy and, as a rule, with more respect than the others. One day a resident, who had mild dementia, was saying she wanted her water pill; she came to my office and said nobody gave her one. We walked to the nurse's station and the nurse informed me she had 'given her one 10 minutes ago,' talking as if the resident were not there. When the resident heard this, she became furious and raised her voice, saying; 'I want my pill, I did not get it yet.' The nurse then turned and proceeded to yell; 'I gave you your pill, I already told you that.' I said something to the nurse about being abrupt, but still, these are the sort of daily assaults that do not necessarily get reported to anyone, but amount to verbal abuse. I am sure, thereafter, that particular resident understood not to tick off any of the staff for fear of retaliation. Unfortunately this scenario took place way too often. Anyone who has ever been in an abusive situation, verbal or otherwise, will tell you that being snapped at, even once, will convey the message. The message conveyed is this; snapping at some people is effective even if it only happens once because once you've been snapped at, you are fully aware that the person snapping at you is capable of doing that if they disagree with you. For some mild mannered residents, snapping at them just once will make them shy away of requesting almost anything they may need in the future. At times, residents may feel the need to use the bathroom quite frequently, either due to the aging process or medication or even urinary tract infections, and will request frequent trips to go pee. I even received a behavior sheet once concerning a resident getting upset because she had been taken to the bathroom and in five minutes requested another trip there. The staff was frustrated because 'she had been told, repeatedly, she had just been taken to the bathroom already' now I'm wondering if staff is my bladder and can tell me I do not need to go again because they felt I have been enough? How much constitutes enough? These forms of abuse are not sensational enough to make the front page, or any page of a newspaper, but these incidents do make for a poor quality of life for residents. Imagine going from your own home where you are able to do basically as you please, to having to now put up with a bunch of strangers snapping at you almost daily. No one is saying staff has to be perfect, or that they are not allowed an occasional bad day in their lives, but there is no excuse, in my book to be rude and downright mean to a resident. This problem exists in nursing homes all the time, even the so-called 'good' nursing homes. Those daily verbal attacks are reminders that this place is not your home. This form of verbal abuse is humiliating and constitutes mental abuse as well, even though many nursing homes do not always see it as such. The Administrators and nursing staff often try to dismiss it as 'a person having a bad day,' but this is more than that to the resident who has to live here and be a captive audience. The horror stories concerning neglect and abuse is just another reason contributing to why elderly fear nursing homes more than death. At least in death, no one can hurt you anymore. We like to think of nursing homes as places of compassion, where caring people work. Unfortunately, some staff people, including some nurses, are there simply for the paycheck. I think, in this bad economy where the most jobs are in the medical field, this rings all too true. If anyone thinks customer service in the retail and restaurant industry has gotten bad, it has gotten even worse in nursing homes. If I have bad service in a restaurant, I have a bad evening. A bad day in a nursing home can mean I have a bad month, year, or life. Probably not a week goes by when we cannot find an article concerning some form of abuse in nursing homes someplace in America. Those are only the ones big enough to make it to the public eye. Is this what you want for your grandmother, father, mother, or even for yourself when old? If the situation is not remedied soon, it will only snowball. There is no reason why every single nursing home across America cannot change for the better, except for laziness on the part of owners and corporations. I cannot begin to tell you how much I despised those corporate trainings we were forced to go to. Those meetings were where, the older I got, and the more I noticed it reminded of the military. Corporations love the younger Social Workers because they would go by corporate policy like it was the Holy Bible. Whatever corporate policy was, those young Social Workers could quote it almost word for word and almost never question its contents. I got so sick of hearing 'our policy is' that I would raise my hand and ask, many times, why the policy had certain phrases in it. I was always told 'that's just the way it is' until I wanted to scream "Why are you not asking why it' this way." The corporations love young Social Workers, not because they are stupid, because they are not stupid in any way. Like the military, corporations and owners the love young Social Workers because most have never worked in a nursing home before, they usually are fresh out of college, and the corporation can mold them to be corporate people simply because they don't know anything else. The young ones also have not become jaded to how their residents are being treated in those places.

Nursing home nurses can be Scary People Sometimes

There are some nurses working nursing homes who are caring and compassionate people, unfortunately they are usually few and far between. For the most part, many of them say and do things that are what I could only describe as 'scary.' For example; the DON of the nursing home decided a woman with dementia was a 'disruption' and needed to go out for a psychological evaluation because she kept removing her shirt in the hallway. This concept of going out for psych evaluations always made me cringe because if people have dementia, going out for a psychological evaluation usually meant the facility wanted them drugged. Why anyone with dementia would need a psych evaluation is beyond me. I had to make arrangements for this because the Administrator and DON were adamant about 'sending her out.' When the resident returned to us, the hospital where she had been sent for a psych evaluation called from their Social Services department and said this lady would remove her clothes when she perceived she needed to use the bathroom. Again, this observation may have been noticed if there were permanent assignments given to staff. When I relayed this observation to the Director of Nursing (DON) her comment was; "Why would she take off her shirt to go to the bathroom?" People with dementia, as mentioned previously, remember bits and pieces of how tasks they used to perform are carried out. A person with dementia will 'remember' something has to be removed to use the bathroom but cannot always recall what article of clothing is removed. Since the shirt was the only clothing she had easy access to, she probably felt, in her own mind that the shirt needed to come off. She was not able to verbalize any longer what she wanted or needed. The fact the DON made such a remark made me think she expected dementia residents to 'understand and think normally' in every situation. This was a scary concept to me because each and every staff person has training in understanding dementia and nurses should have extra training in it simply by virtue of their nursing license. This is the sort of example that tells me many nurses do not take time to get to know residents either. These are not the kind of people whom I want to care for me when I am old and are probably only nurses for the paycheck alone, nothing more. Many nursing homes rely too heavily on mind altering drugs to control people's behavior, especially dementia when it has been proven these drugs do nothing for dementia. All the drugs do is control a person for convenience of staff. Those drugs do nothing to improve a good quality of life for the resident using them. Whenever residents were ordered the powerful psychotropic drugs it was usually because a resident had dementia and was combative. Residents with dementia sometimes become combative and cannot help it when they strike out, usually due to confusion or being afraid of not knowing what is happening to them. Extra staff for dementia residents works much better and is healthier for the resident than psychotropic medications.

A couple of other incidents in the nursing home concerned me as well. One of them involved an elderly woman and her husband who, at the time had been residing in the facility for 10 years. At one of their care plan meetings the husband mentioned that every night after dinner, his wife had chest pains when she tried to lay down for bed. The nurse attending the meeting said she would request an order from the doctor for medicine for indigestion. A few nights later the woman was rushed to the ER and she died of a massive heart attack. From most of the literature about women and heart attacks, the symptoms can masquerade as heart burn. The second incident also involved an elderly woman who was overweight and sedentary. I came to work one morning to find out she had gone to the ER and subsequently died from complications of diabetes. This woman was not on insulin and nurses said they had no clue she was even a diabetic. These two incidents scared me because I began to wonder how these medical conditions could just slip past nurses and doctors. Is it because they were elderly and the medical doctors see no need for tests because of their ages, or is it due to nurses not spotting signs and symptoms. Both of these incidents might have been avoided if staff were given more permanent assignments. Perhaps staff, with a more permanent assignment, might have picked up on subtle changes in those women's conditions, I do not know for sure, but both incidents are scary to say the least. Those incidents did little to exude confidence in a traditionally run nursing home. If families think their loved ones need another opinion and do not like answers given at care plan meetings, they need to inquire further and maybe even obtain another medical opinion. I do not care how old anyone is, everything possible should be done to ensure a person's health is taken care of. The first woman should have been given an EKG to rule out heart disease and the second one should have been given a diabetes test due to the fact of being overweight and sedentary in her lifestyle. As mentioned before, most often the LPN's and the RN's hired in nursing homes are often sub-standard compared to those hired by hospitals. This is usually due to nursing homes wanting to preserve their bottom lines. Private owners have less cash flow to work with, and corporations have to show a profit for stock holders. In either case, saving money and making a profit can translate to short changing the residents of the facility in many ways. If wages were increased, nursing homes would be able to attract a higher quality of worker which would translate into higher quality of care for those living there. Better care would also result in less abuse and less cutting of corners concerning goods and services. The really good nurses in nursing homes are few, they exist and when they are found they generally the ones who are expected to do a good share of the work, making them exhausted. Whenever a person from my department would answer a call light and a resident needed something, usually the nurse at the station would tell us it would get done as soon as an aid was available. This is ridiculous, at best. Nurses are trained to do the same tasks nursing assistants can do, and then some. This is a sign of lazy nursing when they think they are there to do mostly paperwork and nothing else, except dispense some medications once in a while. The facility where I worked had probably three really good nurses and the director of nursing was not one of them. This particular facility was only concerned about the bottom line and so was the administrator. This was a place where the term 'team player' only meant you were in the pocket of the administrator, I saw many good people who had been there for years, go out the door like smoke. The administrator never got it, the owner never got it, and probably still do not get it to this day. It is a sad thing when people are a commodity and the bottom line is valued way above customer service in nursing homes.

Sometimes I envied the nursing department as theirs was a cut and dried and black and white world, pretty much. Medical training does not have as many shades of gray as Social Work tends to have. If a resident did not fall blindly into place in attitudes and behaviors, once entering the nursing home, then it was a problem for Social Services. Nurses were best dealing with that ache Susan has, or the loose bowels Marvin is dealing with. Sometimes I envied their neat, tidy and medically ordered little world of mostly black and white problems. Problems that seemed to be easily solved with this pill or that shot, into the correct area of the body. It is a bit harder to heal a person's mind and soul when this new, strange place does not resemble home or even look anything like a home should be.

Consistent training for nursing assistants is needed

The requirements, including specific ages and training for nursing varies widely from state to state. There needs to be a more uniform code of regulations that every state should have to make training more equal. In Indiana a nursing assistant course consists of three weeks. In New York, where I was a nursing assistant for a time, the course offers a stipend amount of money and consists of a six week course. A six week course is more appropriate because it is more extensive and nursing homes will get a higher quality of nursing assistant because they feel well trained and confident. A three week course is not nearly enough to neither teach anyone nor prepare them for what to expect when on the job. The course I took was part classroom training and later on, training on the floor with a registered nurse a mentor. A six week course also helps weed out people who are not serious enough to continue with the training, thus helping to weed out those who may not be suited for this kind of work. I was dumbfounded with the differences in attitudes in Indiana nursing assistants as compared with New York ones. Those in Indiana had more of a sense of the caring for elderly people was a task and did not necessarily even view the residents as individuals. In Indiana there is a shortage of nursing assistants and the facility where I worked had a very big turnover of nursing assistants. Nursing assistants who are not well trained are more likely to steal from residents and are more prone to abuse of residents who may be difficult to care for. Sometimes the staff where I worked in Indiana even talked about how they felt justified whenever they would argue with a resident. This makes me wonder if staff might have the same feeling of justification if they were rough with or even slapped a resident. This sort of attitude is not a good one for caregivers to have. Many times I would hear staff talking about a new nursing assistant who had been hired and worked the night shift or evening shift, quitting, this was due to, according to other aides, the attitude of the night supervisor who apparently was hard to deal with, herself. I heard nurses talking about how a nurse aide would or should 'toe the mark' on her shift and many nurses treated aides with disrespect and acted superior over them. Caregivers have a job that in itself is stressful and do not need managers to make the job even more stressful. In America we have always had a priority problem, especially where human lives are concerned. I wonder just how much rocket science owners of nursing homes need to have to figure out better pay probably equals out to better quality of staffing. Nursing homes, especially for profit ones, offer up a lousy $6, $7, even $8 and sit around and wonder why staff, who may endure abuse from residents with dementia, leave for better paying jobs. Facilities hire too few aides for too many residents and wonder why the quality of care is not the best and why there is such a high turnover of staff, especially aides. All the while the CEO's of such facilities rake in astronomical paychecks for doing little or nothing to justify their pay. I would not particularly, want a disgruntled aide, who is paid nothing, to take care of me or anyone one I love, daily. This country has always had a major priority problem in that a car's door handle is worth more than a human life, so car workers are paid way more than they are worth and are offered better benefits than someone caring for a human life does. This has always been my big bitch in social work concerning how Christian people always like to consider themselves in this country while showing little compassion and even disregard, for human lives. Many states hire nursing assistants as young as 16 years old which, in my book is way too young. A good case in point was an article on the Internet concerning two young nurse aides in Minnesota who were up on charges of abuse to elderly residents in a nursing home who had dementia. The young women were accused with pinching, slapping, spitting in the mouths of the elderly residents and many other despicable acts against the elderly. This is not only a good example of hiring aides that are too young, but it is also a good testimony of why all states should have the same criteria for nursing assistant training. If the training were consistent in every state, all having higher standards, and the training is extensive, perhaps this sort of abuse could be curtailed.

In service trainings need to be much better than many states and facilities adhere to. More clinical training and longer clinical need to be required by all states to be sure the training keeps up with the needs of today's residents. Nursing assistant is a burn out job and there needs to be more of an effort directed towards teamwork and mentoring. There needs to be more counseling services offered to all nurse aides, both seasoned ones as well as new ones. State and federal inspectors need to be sure all facilities are keeping up with the in service trainings. I have seen some facilities who will mark that employees have had in service trainings when, in fact this is not true, the records get fudged all the time. Inspectors need to be sure the trainings are efficient and are effective, perhaps by increasing the hours of clinical training offered.

Nurse aides are the front line workers in all nursing homes and are often the first ones to recognize any significant changes in a resident's behavior or condition. Nurse aides are pretty much the eyes and ears of any good facility. Their duties need to be more consistent because the scope of their duties can not only vary among states, it can also vary among facilities existing within each state.

Nurse aides need to act in a professional manner, no matter what, and believe me, this is not always the case in many states or in many facilities. Nurse aides need to be able to handle many psychological situations that residents might experience. This is not always the case, as a Social Services Director I had many behavior sheets handed to me concerning things that were not, in any way shape or form, a behavior. Places I worked, many times, were used to handing any situation to the Social Workers situations that could've been best handles on the spot by nurse aides if they were better trained. Consistent training and diligent reviews by nurses trained to do so would help facilities address any areas of weaknesses and help the aides feel more confident by offering more training in the weak areas. Oversight and enforcement of trainings are always left up to each state, but the federal agencies should have more inspectors going out to be sure the trainings are keeping up with federal guidelines.

With hospitals releasing elderly residents much sooner than in previous years, nursing homes are now required to provide care that was usually provided in hospital settings. Nurse aides are faced with more difficult medical and psychological conditions than in previous years. If the guidelines were more stringent, as well as the training, for nurse aides, then facilities would be much more enjoyable for residents. With stricter training more nursing homes could encourage aides to make many decisions on their own without wasting precious time of nurses and Social Workers for situations that could be handled by the well trained aides.

What Are the Practices Nursing Home Staff Label 'Behaviors?'

Let's take a good look at what is considered a 'behavior' in many traditional nursing homes and how those behaviors are usually dealt with. In the nursing home, where I worked in Indiana, I was soon to discover that a behavior was almost always anything that staff did not like, or any performance by a resident that annoyed someone, or anything that got in the way of staff getting tasks done in a timely fashion. In other words; whatever annoyed staff in almost any way imaginable. If a particular resident was not a favorite of the staff person caring for them, then nearly anything that resident did that was unusual, was labeled a behavior, or deemed a habit to be broken in the staff's eyes. Personally, I liked many of the behavior people because it meant, to me, they just refused to take any crap from staff. I saw it as an attempt at having things go their way for a change instead of the institution always calling the shots for them. I recall one lady who was on the assisted feed side of the main dining room, and she started to yell at one of the nurse aides who had been trying to get her to eat something she hated. The aide grabbed her wheel chair and parked her outside the main dining room, which was by my office. I went out of the office to see what was going on and the resident smiled, took my hand and said: "I got my ass kicked out of the dining room." The resident was all smiles and you could tell she was having a wonderful time, knowing she had 'stirred things up in there', in her words. This woman was an apparent thorn in the sides of staff, but I found her to be utterly delightful in her attitude. In fact staff was so paranoid about behaviors; I was given a behavior sheet concerning a man who had never exhibited any behaviors before, 'touching an aide's boobs' on this day. When I delved into the report further, I learned the man had touched her boob while she was transferring him from his chair to a wheel chair. The man had accidentally brushed her boob because he was steadying himself so as not to fall. This was a good example of staff blowing behaviors way out of proportion many times.

Another good example of how behaviors bugged staff involved the laundering of people's clothes. When Susan came to St. Barley's to live, she brought with her some very pretty and expensive articles of clothing. Right off the bat, administration had a shit fit over this because the washing machines used in most nursing homes are industrial strength. Industrial strength, meaning they destroy clothes, so anyone is probably expected to bring their worst, beat up clothing, if they don't want anything nice destroyed.

The use of industrial strength washers and dryers is so blatantly disrespectful of residents and their clothing that it tells people their clothes are no longer important, now they are old. This former attitude is ridiculous, to say the least because I wonder at what age I no longer like nice things anymore, or are not entitled to have them. The Administrator and director of Nursing told me I had to talk to Susan and tell her she should not have brought expensive clothing to wear. I was also to talk to her concerning the habit she had of hanging her pants up in her bathroom to dry once she soaked her undergarments. This habit annoyed staff and the DON said it was unsanitary since she, of course, had a roommate. After all, St. Barley's could not very well be expected to treat her clothing as special; there is no time for that crap. St. Barley's is glad she is well off, has money to pay out of pocket each month and will gladly accept her payments. But do not expect to be treated as an individual in return. I talked to Susan and simply asked her about hanging her pants up in the bathroom and I told her I was simply here to help and see if there was anything we could do to help her. Susan immediately began to cry, indicating to me, the nursing staff, including the aides, had been badgering her about hanging her pants in her bathroom. According to Susan, who was very much in her right mind, the aides kept telling her the habit of pants in the bathroom hanging, wet with urine, was a disgusting practice. All Susan deciphered from those remarks was that she was disgusting and this upset her very much. She felt she had to explain to me she was a neat and clean person, she just did not want her nice clothes ruined in our washers. She even said she was sending her clothing out each week to the local dry cleaners to be washed in a kinder, gentler way, but the cost was very high.

When I heard this, I was quite upset and proceeded to talk to the DON who became totally indignant because I said it bothered me that Susan was in tears due to being made to feel like she was a disgusting person by staff's remarks. The DON was furious at my saying so, and the next thing I knew I was being called to the Administrator's office to explain myself. My explanation to her was I simply was trying to help find a solution to the problem, which I felt should not have been a problem anyway, even though I did not say as much to the Administrator because I knew she just did not care anyhow. All the DON and Administrator saw was that I had the nerve to verbally attack the nursing staff, which, according to nursing homes, can do no wrong. Apparently making a resident feel bad about themselves is fine, if nursing staff does it, or the law according to nursing home rules.

If the damn nursing home had private rooms, if staff were faster to help a person change their undergarments before the resident was soaked, and if there were real washing machines and dryers for residents' clothes, all of this could have been avoided. The nursing home should have changed but, instead, the facility expected the resident to change and conform to the institution. But it snowballed into something ridiculous and staff saw Susan's simple act of hanging her pants in the bathroom as a behavior and even felt justified to make her feel like she was doing something wrong. If a resident is not very happy about being in this place anyway, staff surely does not need to magnify everything so a resident feels so badly they may become depressed. This is why I say the behavior problems were not black and white, cut and dried. Some behaviors were even, in my eyes, created and blown out of proportion by staff. The funny thing about this kind of situation was that I was supposed to tell Susan she should not have expensive clothes, but, on the other hand, if the resident is fond of old clothing that may look a bit worn, nurses badgered me to call family and get that resident some better clothes. Social Services was never respected, nor listened to by nurses or the Administrator, but apparently we were the only department who could call families about almost anything, even though all departments had an office with a phone in it. We were never listened to when we would suggest ways to help make a resident's life nicer, but we were constantly told by other departments, what we needed to do, for them, the staff, to make staff's job nicer. This is not what Social Service is there for.

St Barley's could actually take the windfall they call profit and turn some of it into nicer washing machines that treat everyone's clothing as special. Yes, this may mean a one million dollar profit instead of two million, but I am sure this will not place the owners in the bread line anytime soon.

The Social Services Department was, of course,

in charge of all behavior complaints, actually if we had a sign on our door saying 'Complaint Department' it would have been more fitting. We were given behavior forms most anytime during a work day and we were supposed to take those complaints, deal with the behavior immediately, and then read them at our morning meetings. The object of reading them to others was to give other departments a chance to assist Social Services with finding a solution to the behaviors. This, sharing of ideas from other departments, almost never happened. There was no teamwork going on. The Administrator's idea of teamwork amounted to 'do as I say because no one really cares about your ideas.' This woman did nothing to encourage cooperation among staff. She found that divide and conquer suited her purpose better. So the Social Services department was solely in charge of finding solutions to most of the behaviors going on. Social Services used to be in charge of abuse complaints too, but after bringing the verbal abuse incidents I witnessed almost daily to the Administrator's attention, apparently way too often, that job was given to the DON who would be more inclined to cover up, or at the very least, gloss over, every incident better. This Administrator made it very clear she was not interested in the truth enough to resolve any findings that may be true.

As a Sociologist I am well aware that everyone has their quirks, some people are just quirkier than others. I want you to imagine, if you will, or think about, a favorite thing you like to do, maybe a habit or even a preferred way of saying something. In our daily lives, at home, nothing much is thought of these habits which have meaning to us and we consider as normal.

Maybe you like to lounge around, especially on weekends, in an old favorite t-shirt or sweat pants or semi-worn out shorts. We all have comfortable clothes, favorite blankets or favorite trinkets that have meaning only to us and are very important to us. What are some of your favorite things, what are some things you love very much in this world? Perhaps some article of clothing that helps you feel relaxed or even creative when working around the house or in your garden. We all have our most precious items, be they clothing, trinkets or an old pair of shoes we love, for whatever reasons.

Some of those rituals are what make us unique as individuals and are habits that bring us happiness and enrich our quality of life simply because we choose them. In a nursing home you are expected to get up at the time staff decides, have your shower when they decide it fits their schedule and to dress in whatever staff considers being appropriate attire. But maybe those old sweats and t-shirt, that may look 'ratty' to staff, have some particular meaning to you and you enjoy wearing them. Well, that is just your tough luck and too bad. Those favorite clothes, looking much worn, are now considered a behavior to be dealt with, and probably a habit to be broken in the staff's eyes. The staff now sees all of this as annoying because they now have to write, and

✽

follow, a care plan addressing the habit you and I enjoyed at home and took for granted. A habit or ritual that does no harm to anyone, but somehow, offends staff, or staff now thinks the state surveyors will write them up for not care planning it because they did try to talk you into wearing something 'nicer.' And, if you are a person with dementia, for heaven's sake do not argue with staff over wanting to wear your favorite, but worn, t-shirt and sweats, as this behavior may get you sent out to be evaluated in a psych ward. The arguing with staff over the outfit has meaning to the person with dementia, but because the dementia has rendered the resident incapable of explaining just why the clothes have meaning, the only communication ability the person has left is to grab onto the clothes and refuse to wear something else. Just because staff has no time to find out why the person with dementia is grabbing onto the item, it is now labeled as a behavior.

Refusing to let the item go back into the closet and refusing to wear something else on this particular day, and grabbing at the item, is now considered to be combative and aggressive behavior. The dementia robs people of the ability to communicate effectively and sometimes people remember bits and snatches of habits and things they used to do, but can no longer remember the whole process. For example; an elderly gentleman in the nursing home would unfasten his pants in front of other residents and staff. This was considered a behavior by staff because they saw it as exposing himself. One day I was watching him in the main dining room, he was by himself and I approached him as he was walking with his pants unfastened. I asked him if I could be of some help and he muttered that he knew the shirt tucks in someplace. What staff considered as him exposing himself was likely nothing more than him remembering he used to tuck his shirt in his pants. He would get the pants and belt unfastened, but that was as far as he could get, remembering only the part about unfastening his pants. The rest of the ritual of tucking the shirt into the pants eluded him entirely. With a more permanent staff assignment, somewhere along the line, his personal staff person would have noticed he was simply trying to do what he normally did before developing the dementia. Most nursing homes have a weekly meeting concerning falls and at least a monthly meeting concerning behaviors. Usually the falls meetings consist of, what can be done to reduce falls, and nurses even are allowed to label some people as 'expected fall' people. No one should be known as having 'expected' falls so this tells you not enough is being done to prevent it. One lady in the nursing home I worked in was always getting out of her wheel chair because she had dementia and would become restless in the chair. Nurses were particularly upset about this lady because she required one on one staff at times, a fact that the DON liked to point out to Social Services because there was just 'not enough staff for one on one.' Needless to say, this behavior became a real problem in the nurse's eyes because hiring more staff just did not fit the budget. Apparently budgets are more important in some nursing homes than a resident's quality of life. Alarms were placed on this lady's wheel chair, which had no meaning for the resident, it was simply a tool used for the convenience of staff to know when she was 'getting up.' The alarm allowed staff to run and persuade, even force her to sit back down. To a person with dementia, an alarm not only has no meaning to them, the sound many times is annoying and they will continue to rise in order to look for the source of the noise, in hopes of turning it off somehow. The alarms, in many cases, only add to the behaviors the staff is trying to eliminate in the first place. If staff would be allowed to take the time to review why a person wants to stand up, maybe the staff needs to walk this person, instead of trying to figure out how to tag this as a behavior, all would benefit. With or without dementia, I certainly do not expect my loved one to wear an alarm, nor have to be tagged with an alarm as if they are a cat with a bell. The use of alarms is a sign of not having enough staff and the facility is hoping an alarm will stretch the staff even further and save the facility owners more money. for human beings of any This gives the idea that residents are a commodity for nursing home owners, be they corporations or private owners, to not have to hire adequate staffing, thus making the owners even richer. This view is not a good one and does not promote a good quality of life at any age. This is also the downfall of not having residents and families sit in on board meetings and giving input into what money should be spent on in order to make for a better quality of life in the facility. Residents need to be asked what activities they want, what foods they like to eat, how their rooms should be set up, all the things that make life enjoyable and feel like it is their home. To fail to include residents when planning anything in a facility amounts to nothing more than putting people in a warehouse. The rule in nursing homes is that residents have the right to be free from restraints, chemical or physical ones. The use of chemical restraints seems to be a favorite method used by most nursing homes to help control a person's behaviors. The staff, especially nurses, is very good at getting doctors to write prescriptions for all sorts of chemical restraints. If a resident does not have a medical reason for the restraint, the nurses will usually make one up. This allows them to ask the doctor for a prescription for a psychotropic medication in order to control a behavior the staff is having a 'problem' with. A very good example is depression. Many residents suffer from depression from being in a nursing home and are not always able to make their own rational decisions due to either dementia or sometimes, certain medications, or just because no one takes time to ask them their opinions. Any of these are often reason enough to be depressed. If a person will not come out of their room, wants to go home, and does not wish to mingle with others or attend activities, it is most always diagnosed as depression and in the medical way of thinking, now warrants a prescription for anti-depression medication. The medication is to assist staff with giving the state surveyors the impression the person is having everything done for their condition that is possible. I have a major problem with medical doctors prescribing psychotropic medications anyway. A British study performed over the course of two years, concluded that 'Alzheimer's patients who are prescribed antipsychotic drugs face a higher risk of death than similar patients not given these medications do' (Science Daily, 2009). This study also found that while short term use of antipsychotic drugs in Alzheimer's patients may be of some benefit, prolonged use of them can have serious side effects. I have worked for mental health agencies with a psychiatrist on staff and I believe psychiatrists are much more qualified at diagnosing and treating mental problems. Medical doctors have very little training in the area of mental disorders and many feel the 'magic pill' in the bottle cures all. Not enough research has been done concerning how some of those powerful, mind altering drugs affect the elderly person. There is not enough research about the elderly simply because most people, on average, have not lived as long in the past as they do now with modern medicine helping people live longer. This is not to say there are not many mental health disorders in nursing homes, because there are. Many mental health disorders go untreated because it is very difficult to obtain mental health services for the elderly in nursing homes. If the quality of mental health services were better addressed in nursing homes, perhaps less psychotropic drugs to control the behaviors would be needed. As it stands to this day, many times medical doctors have to rely on what is reported to them by Social Workers or nurses and are compelled to write prescriptions to control the behaviors of many elderly in nursing homes. Most general practitioners do not have enough training in mental disorders to be able to effectively prescribe the correct medications, or the correct dosage of those medications, for elderly residents. The concept of people living this long is a new one. If more nursing homes worked on changing their environment to accommodate residents to feel more at home, I suspect fewer residents would be suffering from depression. Many elderly, even if they feel there is a problem with their care, will express they do not want to 'get anyone in trouble' for registering a complaint. This is absurd since most nursing homes charge upwards of $5,000 per month just for room and board, or in other words, to occupy their rooms. How many of us can afford $5,000 a month rent for our apartments? Not many, I dare to say. As mentioned before, how would anyone really know if a staff person was just a little more rough with a resident, unless the resident registered a complaint on that issue? Or perhaps that particular staff person might take a little longer than usual to get something the resident asked for, or maybe the staff person will be just a tad more brisk in the care the resident receives. It is understandable why sometimes residents are hesitant, or even downright afraid, to register complaints or concerns about a staff person. Unless we live in the resident's shoes, it is hard for us to comprehend being at the mercy of an employee. This fear of retaliation by staff is just another symptom of residents painfully being aware that the facility is not really their home, thus another contributing factor to feeling depressed. People often feel despondent if they feel powerless and think they have no say over their own environment. This feeling of helplessness and having little or no power can often be mistaken for depression. Many times a resident will perk up if they feel like people are not only listening to them, but having the knowledge that things will change for the better because people care about them as an individual can really raise their spirits. All nursing homes should be trying to strive for reasons for residents to want to stay in the nursing home instead of prescribing anti-depression medications. A resident should never, ever have to 'adjust' to conditions they do not like, nor have to 'tolerate' conditions they do not like. Instead of wondering why the resident is not adjusting well, the staff should be looking at what the facility is doing to make a resident want to stay, and want be living there in the first place. I am sure changing the environment would help to lessen the 'behaviors' and lessen the need for anti-depression medications. The increased use of antipsychotic drugs for people with dementia is a good indicator and a red flag for families, that a facility does not have enough staff for dementia residents. Medicare and Medicaid should issue more money for extra staff instead of the use of these ineffective antipsychotic drugs. If a facility, such as the one I worked in, needs to increase the use of antipsychotic drugs to 'control' behavior, I would seriously question the practice and seriously consider removing my loved one from such a facility. This means the facility does not truly care about the health and well-being of its residents. In the nursing home where I worked there would be QA meetings monthly to supposedly 'improve' the facility. But even as a staff member, the staff was afraid to suggest much because you would be greeted with, at best, being reamed out verbally in front of co-workers, or at worst, being fired, or 'let go' as they liked to say. If a staff member, especially a department head, was afraid of retaliation, how much more so the residents being afraid to make suggestions or complain to the Administrator for fear of being brushed off? This particular Administrator liked to pride herself on being able to save the facility owner money and having the ability, in her mind, to know what residents want and need without ever having to ask residents what they feel they needed. How many of us wish to have our lives, especially in our homes, run by someone else who feels they know more than we do about how we should conduct our lives? I would suspect not many of us at all would be very happy with this notion. Relatives, especially, need to speak up at care plan meetings. Always remember you, the family member, are the expert when it comes to knowing what your loved one wants and what their daily habits and routine are, not some staff person in a nursing home.

The Nursing Home Reform Act, part of the Omnibus Budget Reconciliation Act of 1987, stated that nursing homes should try non-pharmacologic interventions before resorting to pharmacologic agents when addressing problem behaviors among residents. While this is true and as a Social Worker, I was expected to notify nurses about reducing psychotropic medications after a certain period, it does not always work well. Many times nursing staff will take it upon themselves, without notifying Social Services, to increase a resident's psychotropic medication, frequently for their own personal reasons. This means, usually because some 'problem' was reported by an employee on one of the shifts. Nurses look at this strictly from a medical model standpoint and they see no 'big deal' in not telling Social Services. This practice is not only capable of getting Social Services in trouble with state and federal inspectors, but may not be in the resident's best interest, not to mention it usually angers the resident's family because no one notified them.   I have sat in on many care plan meetings with families while nurses sat at the table lying to them about why they were not notified of changes in psychotropic medications for a loved one. Most of the time nursing would do its best to throw Social Services under the bus and blame my department for lack of notification. This happened way too often, even though each unit has forms to jot down any medication changes but the forms were seldom used.

In an ideal world, nurses in facilities are supposed to help find solutions to problem behaviors. Nursing should notify doctors and make sure residents have been examined to eliminate every possible reason a person may be experiencing bazaar behaviors. The resident, especially one with dementia who cannot communicate well, may be having pain of some sort causing the behavior. This rarely happens because nursing does not want any more to do than it absolutely has to, so the first department they all came to was Social Services. Social Workers cannot order tests to be run, x-rays to be run, or any other medical orders. We could only ask nursing to please send the doctor a request, but this rarely was done. You see if a resident did have tests done and something showed up medically, nursing is afraid it looks like they did not do their jobs, even if that was exactly the case. A good example of this was a resident who yelled out all the time. The poor woman was not able to coherently communicate with us and she could only yell out one word all the time. Nursing and administration kept telling Social Services we had to do something, even though nothing medically was ever checked or ruled out. My department notified her family and got the proper paperwork for permission to send this lady for a mental evaluation. While she was in the psych ward of the hospital, it was discovered she had an infection as well as a hip fracture which gave her a good deal of pain. The Social Worker of the psych ward was nice to me on the phone, but said she really was within her rights if she filed a complaint with the state against St Barley's for neglect. I went to the Administrator with this news only to be told that if she, the other Social Worker, filed a complaint, my job was on the line. This kind of wacked out, crazy reasoning is exactly what drives good social workers to resign in nursing home. This woman had been medically neglected because nursing was too swamped or too lazy to have medical tests run first before assuming the behaviors were psychological. It is far easier to get Social Services to send a person for a psych evaluation, even though getting the necessary paperwork and making arrangements to admit a resident to a psych ward, takes a full day on top of the work my department already has. In the eyes of nursing, Social Services does nothing, is not near as important as nursing and has all the time in the world to be at nursing's beck and call. In other words, Social Service is the red headed stepchild with freckles.

I got very tired of behavior reports about residents who 'refused to go to bed at a certain hour,' a resident who would not stay in bed once put there for the night and I really got sick of those who 'were angry when asking for a cookie and became angry with staff 'just because they refused to give them a cookie.' The part that made me the maddest was the word, refused, within the content of the behavior reports. Who in hell is staff to refuse someone anything?

I remember, at one corporate meeting, part of the training consisting of 'how to handle problem residents and their families.' I distinctly remember a younger Social Worker saying: 'Especially those who want to go home against medical advice (meaning not waiting for permission from the doctor or nursing home staff) because 'they probably just want to smoke anyway, so they insist on leaving.' Why was this Social Worker not looking into why some residents just couldn't leave fast enough, instead of considering those residents as a problem? Anything that deviates from the norm, as we see it, or anyone who just isn't adjusting to corporate rules, are deemed as having behaviors, even according to corporate policies. Well, gee, maybe residents need to read everyone's corporate policy, so they can 'fit in.' How utterly ridiculous that would be. I guess it does not always occur to people working nursing homes that people want to leave so they can do as they please, as we all do, even smoking. I am not advocating smoking, but if I smoked all of my life and am now 70 or 80 or 90 years old, I do not expect to be deprived of the few things left, vises or not, that make me happy. Maybe in my younger life, I deprived myself of many things, but in older life, I do not expect to have to deprive myself any longer. This seems perfectly reasonable to me.

I have seen, and grown weary, of staff, doing things, for no other reason than because the corporation says to do it. I see people not questioning anything they do, not requiring a purpose or even just a good reason, for doing certain things. I have seen far too many administrators who are cut from corporate cloth. None of us would even consider entering anyone's home, especially our peers, and dictate to them how they should live their lives, just because we say they should live it a certain way. Yet very few nursing home staff ever even shy away at doing exactly that in a nursing home, to old people. Is it because old people have been so devalued in our society we feel we have the right to do that simply because they are old now? Is it because, while we are younger, we feel we are the only ones who know how life should be lived? Or is it true, that because older people no longer are productive members of society, we can just throw them away? Have we truly become the age of paper plate people, once people are used up, in our eyes, we just toss them away? Especially if those paper plate people remind us of our own mortality? I have seen staff attend corporate trainings and continue to agree with a corporation's policy for no other reason than to stroke the egos of a corporation's top brass, or worse yet, for staff to gain a promotion.

The 9 Inch and Other Stupid Rules

Nursing homes have state inspectors who come in on a regular basis to inspect what is known as life and safety requirements for the facility, or more rules to 'live by' as most employees call it. The inspectors also go to every resident's room to check for any violations of safety laws. I do not know how many of us would appreciate having safety inspectors come into our private homes and do this, but I imagine few of us would like it. While no one is suggesting there should be fire hazards and dangerous situations in nursing homes, but the inspections should not be any different than an apartment building might receive. Unfortunately, in the case of nursing homes, the inspection ends up knit-picking into resident's private lives.

There is the '9 inches rule,' this means a resident should not have anything on their closet shelf that is less than 9 inches from the ceiling.

Come on, how many of us are going to allow an inspector into our private homes to inspect our closet? I dare say, if anyone came into my house and tried this crap, I would kick their ass to the curb in a heartbeat. Why on earth residents in a nursing home should have rules like some prison is beyond me. I have plenty in my home closet and it is stacked clear to the ceiling and I just dare anyone to tell me I cannot do this. Residents were also not supposed to have anything on their closet floors unless it was in plastic totes. Well this is not summer camp, so if you want me to have plastic totes, then you need to provide them, since I pay $5000 a month to live in this place.

I would get calls, almost weekly, from the Administrator or maintenance, telling me I needed to call a resident's family concerning the dreaded nine inches rule, or, concerning the resident having too many personal belongings and they just had to go. Maybe I like to collect things, maybe, as a resident; I already gave up more than half of my items with sentimental value already. The calls concerning too many personal items always pissed me off, I usually asked staff if I needed to come and weed out their personal belongings at their houses, but I never had anyone take me up on my 'offer,' much to my surprise.

The nursing home I last worked in was owned by one family, mostly by a man and his wife. The facility was started in the 1980's and as many of the older workers still working there, liked to say: "That was when it was a nice place to live and work." When I inquired as to this statement, I was informed it 'used to be a small place and staff were more personal.' Unfortunately, as the population grew, along with the owner's greed, it became a place steeped in rules. By the time I became Social Services Director, the owner was no longer concerned about the residents' comfort and happiness, he was concerned with cutting corners and saving a buck. He would make an appearance daily simply to keep an eye on his interests and investments and to make sure his money was 'not being wasted' in any way. In fact, the owner went so far as to hire an Administrator whose expertise was in money crunching to save money. This woman and the facility owner were perfect examples of how not to run a nursing home. None of them were, in any way shape or form, schooled in culture change, or anything, that might make the facility more like home. I was soon on the road to learning that the game the Administrator and owner liked to play was; how much can we get away with before state inspectors or families complain. This game soon turned out to be exasperating to employees; even those who had been there for a long time, and the game was the cause of many staff members finding other places of employment. The new Administrator's way of managing the nursing home staff was authoritarian rule which has 'gone out with the dark ages' as one employee so aptly put it.

For example, the owner had finally agreed with the Administrator, to replace decade's old furniture.

The decision to do this was not about caring for the residents, but more about marketing and appearance because the nursing home competition had become stiffer in recent months. The owner needed all the help he could get to attract more residents. He was so concerned about his investment that he went so far as to post rules and regulations for the residents to 'live by, or adhere to,' as he liked to put it when I asked him about them. The rules went like this; Residents will be quiet during activities (kindergarten anyone?), so as not to disturb other residents and residents will leave the Main Dining room as soon as activities are over Residents will practice good hygiene and will maintain proper attire when out of their rooms. Residents will not lie down on the new furniture not put their feet on any of the new furniture.

The bulk of the new furniture was placed in the nursing home lobby, to look nice for people taking tours, and the rest in the units where mostly short-term residents stayed who had come for therapy. Those who came just for therapy were paying the facility with Medicare, which meant a higher rate, which translated to the owner as people who were worth more, or were more important in his eyes. The owner did not feel long-term residents were entitled to new furniture because many were on Medicaid and nor reimbursing the facility at as high of a rate. Never mind those who paid out of pocket, and even those on Medicaid paying for longer and supporting the operations of the place longer.

Those posted rules broke every violation of residents' rights in the book as far as I was concerned and had no place in a home where adults live. The rule concerning hygiene absolutely did not apply because it was staff that made sure residents were clean and well dressed. Older people, for the most part, are only living in a nursing home because they need some sort of assistance with day to day activities. Rules concerning activities were absurd because the activities are so awful in most nursing homes, it is almost impossible to attract very many residents as it is, without creating rules to deter the few who do show up for any of those boring events.

One of our residents used to enjoy sitting in the front lobby charging his wheel chair while looking out the windows. One day, the Administrator, came to my office and informed me she did 'not like him doing this' because it just did not look nice in her eyes. She told me I must talk to him about not doing this anymore. She said the staff was responsible for charging his chair and I was to tell him he did not need to do it anymore. There was absolutely no harm in this man sitting in the lobby charging his wheel chair. I refused to inform him of the things she wanted me to and from then on, it was her custom to be critical of anything I did concerning my job since I was not 'cooperative' to bait and fetch for her every request.

Another problem the Administrator seemed to have, and brought to my attention, was residents who liked to have Christmas trees up in their rooms well after the holiday was over. This seemed to bug her, yet at one morning meeting, she told us all about her Christmas tree in her home which remained up year round. Apparently this practice was fine for an

Administrator who lives in the community, but not fine for residents of her prison system. She informed me I had to call families of those with the trees and tell them they needed to take the trees down. I flat out refused to do this task either, explaining to her about residents' rights. The owner told me, later in the day, it is not the residents' facility, and he built it and maintains it, so it is his facility.

We live in a new era, an era where Administrators and owners, like those, should be obsolete. That kind of thinking, shared by those two, should have no place in today's nursing homes. In this day and age of competitiveness in nursing homes, smart corporations and owners of these facilities will want to usher in culture change. Culture change is the term used for the complete changes that really good nursing homes usher in. All nursing homes can and should be ushering in culture change because it not only is good for people who work and live there, but it is becoming the way of the future, if they hope to stay in business for very long.

Staff in nursing homes have to adopt the mindset that this is a person's home and how any staff person chooses to run their own homes has no bearing on how the nursing home should be run. The nursing homes should be run mostly by what residents want in their personal lives, not scheduled around the facility's routine or time tables or for the convenience of the staff. Obviously nursing homes need to stop being obsessed by rules and regulations, made up by Administrators as they go along to cover their own personal annoyances or ushered in by a corporation calling the rules corporate policy.

The place I worked, in Indiana, had a new Administrator who had worked in another facility for 18 years. It always puzzled me why she would leave a job after so long being employed there. Places have been known to 'offer' to allow an Administrator to resign rather than being fired in order to save face; sort of 'passing the trash' I believe industry leaders refer to it as. Maybe her authoritarian style of administration no longer suited the former nursing home where she used to work, so she came to a smaller one where she could better practice the style. Especially since

the owner obviously shared her ideas about who

is in charge and who 'runs' the place. The owner

admitted to me he has been sued by former employees

and residents in the past for some of the 'politically

incorrect' ways of handling situations.

How nursing homes usually rid themselves of troubling residents by abusing the discharge system

Another thing many nursing homes do is rid themselves of residents, especially Medicaid residents, by deeming them as unsafe or claim the facility might not be appropriate for their particular needs. The translation of this is; the resident is costing us more money than we receive in Medicaid reimbursement especially when the resident is causing too much trouble for staff. Once Medicare expires, Medicaid residents become less profitable and less desirable to a facility. Where I worked as Social Services Director, my department was expected to talk with residents and families and let them know we did not take 'Medicaid pending' residents. To the owner and administrator, this was a 'sound business practice' to me it was abhorring because neither the owner nor administrator ever had to tell residents and families this fact; it was shoved onto social services. Nursing homes will deny they do this, but they do it, and quite often. The procedure involves staff members writing up incident reports in order to have a paper trail, which looks like staff is so concerned over the resident's safety and well being. One case scenario in the place I had worked was a case concerning a woman who lived in the facility for several years and had developed dementia over time. This particular woman took to wandering into other resident's rooms and would take items off of the med carts (another good reason to do away with med carts). The woman had been living in the facility for several years as a self-paying resident. When her money ran out, her family had to apply for Medicaid to pay for her stay. Once the woman began being a problem the facility really did not want her there because nursing homes do not get reimbursed at a high enough rate, so for the staff to have problems with anyone they feel it is just not worth their while. At the high cost of nursing home care, most people will probably have to apply for Medicaid at some time during their stay, and if a resident is there long enough, it is very likely they will develop dementia in some form. The facility where I worked was worried (mainly the director) about the state surveyors giving them a ding if the woman happened to get into something while they were there, or another resident's family might complain, which in any case, would be too much trouble. Since this woman's family refused to allow her to take any psychotropic medications (which most research indicates does not work for dementia anyway), the facility decided to do everything in its power to send her to another nursing home, if possible. The family was certain the facility only wanted to be rid of her as a problem because she was on Medicaid, but the facility presented documentation to try and prove to the state it was in the resident's best interest to move. Facilities will chart all incidents they deem as a behavior over a period of time, and if there is a hearing, will present this trumped up evidence to prove they are right to request a move. This is very difficult for families to fight since the state usually considers nurses as experts who know what is best for residents. All of the evidence concerning this particular woman was formatted by mostly nursing staff, and if the woman had remained self-pay I imagine her problematic behavior would have been tolerated much more. Another woman in the facility was having mental health issues and took to saying mean things to staff and also began mistrusting staff members. Eventually the administrator decided the family needed to be convinced that the woman should go to a psychiatric facility so it was up to staff to get the family, her daughter mostly, to agree. Neither women were really a threat to anyone, residents nor staff, but both presented too much trouble because staff was beginning to complain about having to deal with both residents. There are usually only six reasons a resident can legally be evicted from a nursing home. Those six reasons are; if the resident is well enough to go home, need special care only available elsewhere, are a danger to the health of other, endanger the safety of others, fail to pay their bills, or the nursing home closes. This practice of getting rid of residents on Medicaid, who present some sort of problem, or who require a high level of care, is absolutely appalling at best, and sneaky and underhanded at worst. Moving the elderly resident to a new facility can be devastating to them. Moving for any of us is a stress, but to the elderly, this kind of stress can have dire consequences, such as depression, weight loss, and posing a high risk of falls for them. If anyone thinks their loved one is being shoved out of a nursing home because they are problematic and on Medicaid, they are likely not far off the mark. The facility I worked at is not the only nursing home that does this practice by any means. Nursing homes that used to be mostly privately owned are increasingly being bought up by corporations who have to 'show a profit' continually to their stockholders. Corporations have increasingly seen the profit potential in the frail elderly population and are building virtual empires. Nursing homes constantly send the admissions people to hospitals to snag people who can be discharged early into nursing homes. Nursing homes can then utilize Medicare funds by offering a vast array of therapies to promote recovery. Larger more profitable nursing homes have compromised care by understaffing, keeping tight control of the food costs and curtailing any improvements such as culture changes, which are not as profitable. To many large chains, size has become a hindering factor because of more people demanding culture change. Nursing home care, to be humane, has to be a highly individualized affair. When too many residents of a diversified population; frail elderly mixed with dementia and sub acute care (those only needing therapies) are under one roof of a nursing home, someone is going to get neglected due to under staffing. Most of the time it is the frail elderly and the dementia residents who suffer neglect. The sad thing in all of this is the lovely brochures showing a trusting resident gazing into the eyes of a caregiver, while the caregiver holds their hand. Another sad fact is that many administrators claim, and probably believe, they are experts when it comes to giving compassionate care to the elderly. This, for the most part, is not so. The frail elderly and dementia residents often get neglected due to under staffing because the sub acute care residents are more alert and can voice their needs much better, so they get their needs met quicker. The attempt to provide a wider range of services to a wider population under one roof, does not work well at all. Too many resident to resident assaults take place and too many wandering residents tend to escape and with dire consequences, especially in inclement weather conditions. If a resident becomes combative, wanders too much, needs a high level of medical care, gets medications that cost too much or in general is a problem in any way, it is likely a facility will do all in its power to dump the resident if they receive Medicaid. This amounts to another form of elder abuse, subtle as it may be. This is why Medicaid and Medicare need to put more money into extra staff for a facility, not more money into psychotropic drugs that do nothing for dementia residents anyway. In the economic hard times that all states are facing most recently, many states want to trim health care and Medicaid costs. With so many more elderly needing nursing home care, this is not the time to cut back Medicaid funds because nursing homes are struggling as it is when Medicaid is not paying near enough to help the frail elderly.

There is a massive crisis going on in state after state concerning the care and funds for the frail elderly population. Little attempts by governments have been made to address the waste of resources and the exploitation of elderly needing nursing home care. While private owners and CEO's of corporate for profit nursing homes, are paid huge salaries and rake in huge profits, they will continue to offer sub-standard care to save a buck and preserve the bottom lines.

More changes need to be made, someone has to stand up and speak for the frail elderly, many of whom do not have a voice due to major illnesses or dementia, and many have no family to speak out for them. We, as a society, need to remember we all get old and when we see how most nursing homes are run, we need to ask ourselves if we would be happy in them should we ever need their care. If we continue to answer no, and the community continues to fear ever having to go to a nursing home, then people need to stand up and protest this sort of care. Nursing cannot continue to be run like fast food chains and the frail elderly should not continue to be viewed as a commodity for executives and private owners of for profit homes to exploit for their own financial gains.

Residents Don't Decide Anything

Another practice in traditional facilities that is a personal annoyance to me is the fact that evening and night staff thinks elderly people should have a bed time. I have done research on this subject and there does not seem to be much written about staff insisting residents have a particular bed time. I suppose, before me, maybe no one has really thought much about this subject. Maybe outsiders have never noticed this is the case in nursing homes. This belief that residents need a bed time tells me that most staff feel like elderly coming into a facility are now two years old and need staff to tell them when to go to bed and when to rise in the morning and when to take a nap. Elderly should be receiving the respect that living the 65, 85, or even the 95 years they have lived warrants them to receive. For all those years as adults, they have decided those things for themselves, and staff members do not need to take that role for the residents. Once a person has come to live in a nursing home, that person is retired. There is no reason, except for staff convenience, for them to be getting up at five or six in the morning. They have no place to be so damned early and no jobs to go to. Retired people have earned the right to set their own schedules. As a Social Services Director I was disgusted whenever I actually received a behavior form stating how a resident just refused to either go to bed at a certain time or refused to stay in bed after being put there. When I was a nurse aide on the 3 to 11 shift, there was a woman whom other aides would put to bed at 8:00, I would answer her call bell at about 9:00PM and she would tell me she could not sleep. I would usually help her get her robe and slippers and walk her up the hallway so she could listen to the soft music on the radio in the nook at the spot near the nurses' station where there was an easy chair and soft lights. As discussed before, having to live in a nursing home can cause insomnia for many residents due to having to adjust to a new environment anyway. Nursing homes can and should, work towards finding ways to reduce noises at night that also may contribute to insomnia in nursing home residents. As an aide I soon discovered the bed time rule was for the convenience of the staff so they could take longer, and more breaks, not for the good of the residents. I say, reserve the bedtime sort of junk for your young children at home, and do not use it on elderly adults. If anyone came into my home and dared to tell me when I need to go to bed, I would smack them upside their heads. Absolutely do not disrespect elderly adults with this sort of suggestion. This rule, like so many others in nursing homes, is absolutely pointless, unless a facility is trying to suck all of the enjoyment out of peoples' lives.

After receiving a behavior report from staff concerning a resident who did not 'stay in bed, or even in his room' once put there, I interviewed him because, fortunately, he was very alert and orientated. He explained to me that when he rang his bell for help, he'd waited for a very long time so he went to the hallway and he admitted to swearing at staff because they seemed to 'be having a party and making a lot of noise' so he figured they were ignoring his bell. When I brought this up with the DON, she said this guy was simply a 'chronic complainer anyway' which brings us back to 'behaviors' of residents who do not make the popular list with staff members anyway. This response is not only absurd, it smacks of disrespect for any resident with a real gripe. No wonder one elderly gentleman once said to me: "I have learned not to think, not to feel, to stop questioning and stop complaining because no one cares to hear about it." There is very little attempt, by staff or administration, to identify or respond to individual's needs or wishes.

While it is true that as people grow older, some people become frail and do need some amount of assistance with daily routines. Older people recognize that a certain amount of dependency is unavoidable. What is most shocking to them when they enter a nursing home is, quite often, being put in the position of feeling complete and enforced, dependency now thrust upon them by staff. As we discussed before, imagine yourself coming to live in a place from your home, where you exercised a certain amount of judgment and freedom in your daily decisions, to now having to be utterly and completely dependent upon staff and the facility's schedule. Simple events like mealtime, bath times, and going to bed, having a cup of coffee and daily activities are no longer events where you are able to exercise much choice.

Imagine, if you can, how demoralizing it must be to experience the endless waiting older people must endure in nursing homes. Waiting to use the bathroom, waiting to take your medicine, especially pain pills, waiting to eat and waiting for assistance when you want to go to bed can destroy your independence.

Institutions probably feel they have done the residents a big favor by removing any decision- making responsibilities and giving them, what they now think is a life of leisure. In fact, what they have succeeded in accomplishing is making residents, slowly but surely, totally dependent upon staff for everything. It is no wonder older people report feelings to Social Services such as, 'feeling useless,' feeling like 'no one listens or cares anymore,' and feeling like their lives are pretty much over. Residents are never even consulted on simple things like a facility's décor.

Residents complain about not being allowed to reach for items on their own closet shelves, if any staff notices them doing so. One resident told me she was 'scolded' for standing by her wheelchair and reaching for an item on her closet shelf. She told me a staff member told her to never do that again, because if she fell, they would get blamed for it. She was not encouraged to do anything, except for menial tasks, like writing, on her own so she felt like she was 'in jail' as she so aptly put it. To most elderly, asking for help is very foreign to them and asking for constant help from strangers, is like having to beg for help all the time. Many elderly have so long been used to being self-sufficient from an early age that if they cannot do it themselves, they will go without rather than having to ask.

When residents enter a nursing home, they are all, no exceptions, expected to conform to the facility's rules. I see no reason why people who are paying so much money to live someplace need to change habits of a lifetime for the convenience of staff or administration in a place.

Staff should be the only ones to ever have to conform or change their habits when entering a facility. Just as all home health care staff is expected to follow the rules in a person's private home, this too, is the residents' home and staff needs to follow the rules in a facility laid out by residents, not vice versa.

Social Services vs. the Golden Children and the Cash Cows of the Nursing Home Business

I ended up at the Social Services Department of the last nursing home I worked in because, at the time, I was an outreach case manager for a new company who landed a state contract working with MR/DD people. This was not a bad job, except the company was new, nothing had been ironed out, like all of the kinks yet, so I felt like I was floundering as to what was expected. Even my supervisors had no clue because this was too new to them as well. Because the job was out in the community, there arose a dispute between management and some case managers over not being paid gas mileage while having to use our own vehicles. We would sometimes have to drive hundreds of miles a week with no reimbursement for gas.

I saw the ad for a Social Services Assistant of the nursing home and, on a lark, I submitted my resume. In two days of their receiving my resume, I was called in for an interview. The Social Services Director was only 26 years old, but very sweet and, as I was to learn, quite good at her job there. For only 26 she was very compassionate and caring of the residents, she possessed a wisdom and understanding far beyond her 26 years. In fact she understood elderly residents better than some people I had known who were twice her age. The initial interview was also my first encounter with the Administrator of St. Barley's. In the Administrator's office, she, not the Social Services Director, ran the interview and put on an appearance of being pleasant, but, even then, I could tell she was somewhat distant to people. Absolutely not a touchy feely type of warm fuzzy personality at all, but I was tired of driving hundreds of miles and this place was 10 minutes from my home. The interview went well and I was hired a week later.

I reported to work and I enjoyed working with my new Director of Social Services because Crystal very was thorough and taught me my end of the job well. If I had any questions, she was more than willing to answer them or show me some way of charting better in order to make state officials happy. The funny thing about the demands of charting and care planning in nursing homes is this; a person goes into social work usually because they like helping people. They like spending time with residents and helping them solve problems. The problem is, you have to spend so damn much time writing that you did this or that for a resident, it ends up being fudged lies because you have to write so many volumes saying what was done, that you usually don't get time to actually do what you claim was done. It ends up being bull shit because it's hard to find time to spend with residents in your care. You don't lie about big things, like abuse reports, but the small stuff. Stuff like weekly supportive visits to people you know need extra conversations and attention. Sometimes the amount of paperwork defied my comprehension and, at times, I felt like social work in a nursing home seemed to be nothing more than pushing and filing endless mountains of papers. In some ways being a social worker in a nursing home is much more frustrating than when I was a nursing assistant or home health aide. This was because as a nurse aide not a lot was expected of you except

the solving of an immediate problem. As an aide
the problems in your realm are smaller and solvable.
Things like helping with a bath a meal, clean linens,
etc. Being a social worker put you in a position where
you appear to be able to solve problems and should
be able to solve problems and residents and families
expect you to be able to. Except now there is such
a mountain of rules and regulations set by state and
federal governments and an administrator who will
not let you do anything on your own, that your hands
are tied. This proved, to me, to be very stressful and
frustrating. In social work, no problem is black and
white nor cut and dried.

When I started the job, little did I know that the
department heads' annual review was taking place.
My new director was called in for hers and she
returned to our department looking pretty upset. I
asked if everything was alright and she said: "The
Administrator says I am not a team player." From
what I had observed she seemed to be very good at
her job, but I was also soon to learn that 'team player'
involved kissing the ass of the Administrator and

Director of Nursing, or DON for short, at St. Barley's. It also soon became apparent that the Social Services department in this nursing home was merely tolerated because the state rules say all nursing homes have to employ a Social Services person, or people, depending upon how many residents live there. Nurses take care of the residents' medical needs and are the Golden Children and therapy brings in loads of money in the short term so they are the Cash Cows. Nursing assistants, housekeeping, custodians and Social Workers are not bringing in money so we are all treated like shit, essentially. Even nursing assistants, who really take care of the residents 24/7, are considered the grunts or slaves to the nurses and get very small pay and even smaller respect, even though they are very needed and essential to day to day operations of the place. Therapy people and nurses sit upon a big throne and are considered to be higher on the food chain than the rest of the employees. Even dietary, or the dietitian, gets more respect than Social Services because, for some reason, food is on a higher plane than a resident's comfort too. The Admissions/

Marketing Coordinator of St. Barley's was also on a high plane, because even though she did not do much, she was in charge of raking in residents, or paying customers. Our facility had a pretty decent reputation in the community so she really did not have do much marketing and we all suspected she was probably out getting her hair or nails done most of the time instead of marketing, because she would be gone for hours at a time. She was well liked by the Administrator because she was a good ass kisser to her, and as much as everyone despised the Administrator, she was basically one of the Administrator's few friends in the building.

We would have morning meetings every day to discuss room changes, who the admissions person was looking at for admissions and essentially, what was happening on the day ahead. The Administrator, as mentioned before, did absolutely nothing to encourage team work among the staff and I think it is safe to say she even pitted some staff members against each other from time to time. Dividing and conquering seemed to suit her purposes well, so she adopted it as her motto. It wasn't long before I noticed that the Administrator, if pissed or annoyed about something she thought a department head had done, or not done, would rip them a new one in morning meeting in front of their co-workers. She would do this in a loud voice and never allow the person being attacked to explain why something did or did not happen as the Administrator thought it should have. This was a really piss poor way of running anything but it was to let staff know she thought of the rest of us as a much lower class than herself and reminded us, in no uncertain terms who was in charge of the place. She ruled using fear and intimidation, which made it hard for most of the employees to concentrate on their jobs because they were always in fear of being fired. And she also had to micromanage every department, never trusting department heads enough to make any decisions without her approval. She even went so far as to have our whole inner office phone system replaced with what she claimed was a more modern one. She claimed it would be more efficient, I knew better once I saw it. The new system, with its 'out of office' button we were required to push if out of our office and the phone history memory option showing every phone call out and into an office daily, was just one more way to micromanage, or spy on the staff. Another motto the Administrator had was; 'if this employee does not kiss my ass, there's more where they came from, who will kiss it.' Many of our morning meetings would bring contempt and anger upon the Social Services Director because we would be handed behavior sheets at these meetings. Social Services was expected to be much more than Social Workers, we were to be magicians, fixing behaviors, psychologists for residents as well as for staff problems, to be the bearers of bad news or to let residents and families know the rules because the Administrator expected us to be her lackeys whenever she was not happy with rule breakers. I noticed the Administrator, quite often, singled out our department, namely the Director, for doing something wrong, or for not doing enough to change a behavior. If anyone was having a behavior, she would often say; "Well send them out." Meaning, get rid of the problem, the sooner the better. She did not care there was a procedure involved in getting anyone admitted to psychiatric services and had little interest in ever knowing the procedure.

I was working there for three months when the Social Services Director told me she was starting to look for a position elsewhere. I was not thrilled about this because, had I known she might be leaving soon, I might have had second thoughts about accepting the position of Assistant. She kept sending out her resume and finally landed an interview at the local college. The Administrator acted like she was absolutely stunned and acted clueless as to why the Director might not be happy here. The poor director was taking Prozac in order to be able to tolerate the Administrator and to 'find the enthusiasm to come to work each day.' This was one of the first, in what would be a long line, of competent people the Administrator succeeded in driving out the door while I worked there.

Between the Administrator being harsh and

always holding the club of 'you will be fired for nothing' over her head and the DON being a total bitch and trying to run the Social Services Department, it just proved too much for my Director to take anymore. I did not blame her, no one should have to swallow Prozac daily just to be able to report to work and function amid overbearing stress.

While a new job was very nice for the former director, it turned to be the beginning of a bad situation for me. The Administrator decided any monkey off the street could be the Social Services Director, and although I applied for the position and was trained and experienced, she decided she wanted someone who would blatantly kiss her ass, right or wrong, qualified or not. Most of the candidates interviewed leaned towards the not qualified category, fresh out of college, no experience with elderly or anyone else and thought they could jump in and know how to run our department. I got to sit in on interviews, as well as the present Director, which was stupid because I would be the one working with anyone new, not the Director who was leaving anyway. While I may have been asked to sit in on interviews, the Administrator never asked my opinion and made it clear she did not care what it was. She ended up hiring the first candidate, I say first because there proved to be many in succession, based upon the recommendation of one of the nurses. I figured this candidate might not be too bad because since a nurse had recommended her, then we would be thought of on a higher plane and maybe our department might be doing everything right instead of wrong, based on her friendship with the elite class. On the day of orientation, this person who was hired, sent an email to the Administrator saying she had 'changed her mind' about the job and was not going to show up after all.

The Administrator was so pissed about this that she decided to drag her heels when it came to hiring another person. The day came and went when the Director was to be done and still no one had been hired. I guess the Administrator figured why pay two people, no hurry, when they could work one person, me, to death and save money. After all, this nursing home, like most others, was all about profit not truly caring for residents. I ended up, for several months, serving both unite, all 108 residents, more or less, by myself. I had a part-time helper, an older Social Worker who had been there for over 20 years. When I started working there she explained she had retired twice but came back to work twice when they needed someone to fill in at the front desk and has been working the front desk every weekend for the past few years. She would come to Social Services twice weekly, Friday and Monday and work for a few hours. She had no clue about putting data into a computer, so she could not do that, but was able to do other, time consuming tasks, such as interviewing recent admissions and charting the information. But, for the most part, I was thrust into doing most of the social work all by myself.

What also made it even more fun was the fact it was spring and this was the time the state surveyors were due to come in and check our books and inspect how the place was being run. Surveyors are a ragtag lot because they never look for the same thing in every facility and never give a damn either about if the facility resembles anyone's home. They look for dust over a door jam, if anyone got psych services was the paperwork correct? Were the residents getting their meals with the correct number of hours in between each one? Most of what they look for is stupid and institutional-oriented anyway. Just before the state shows up, there is a frenzy of making sure things are 'done right' and data is up to date in charts and most of the entire sacred state book where surveyors look for updated data from each department. Most of this crap is never worried about the rest of the year, but now, due to inspections coming up, it makes employees run around like chickens with their heads cut off.

I ended up coming in at six in the morning and working until five or six every evening from a week until the surveyors show up until they are done with the inspections, which was two weeks later due to the fact this year they are two people short, two who either retired or quit. Not one time do the surveyors care if anyone has a private room, or a place to make tea, coffee or snacks, it is inspected like the institution that it is run as.

After a series of losers being hired and tested by the Administrator for the position of Social Services Director, she calls me in to her office, via email, to talk to me. The Administrator rarely comes out of her office so if you are summoned to her office, it is via email or she will buzz you on the phone. This woman is grossly overweight, so it felt like I was going to see Jabba the Hutt in the Creature Cantina every time I was summoned.

She motions for me to sit down and proceeds to tell me 'no one has worked out in the position because either the staff does not like the former candidates or she did not like them.' Staff not liking those meant nurses did not like them, usually translated as the people did not kiss ass to the Administrator or to the DON. The Administrator then asks me if I will be willing to accept the position. Now this, mind you, is weeks after I work my ass off with 12 hour days and her believing all, that time that she can find some kiss butt to groom to walk on residents' rights for her. That, in a nut shell is how I took on the position of Social Services Director, one of the most thankless positions there. Director of a department that is merely tolerated and is expected, for the most part, to be a messenger or an extension of the Administrator and nursing and to do their dirty work for them so they don't need to look bad.

In most traditional nursing homes, nurses working there do not tend to be the cream of the crop, either in their schools or in their field. Nursing homes tend to attract the inferior batches of the lot mostly because shoddy, inferior sub-standard nursing is tolerated much more in nursing homes. In fact LPN's who present inferior work show up in droves. It is a known fact among nurses that it is easy to get away with illegal activities in most nursing homes. It is not uncommon for nurses to be able to write prescriptions for drugs for their (the nurses') own use or extra prescriptions to sell on the black market. This sort of thing happens more often than most people realize. In fact, one other nursing home I had worked, the pictures were often stolen right off the walls on some weekends and no one noticed it or reported it. Many times nurses were let go because they would show up drunk too often, or had asked doctors for prescriptions that their resident did not need. Nurses could count on getting away with this kind of behavior for a long time. I suppose most who were caught thought they could keep asking for bogus prescription indefinitely. The pay is so crummy in nursing homes that the higher quality of nurses does not exactly stand in line to work in long-term care settings.

Where I worked, the DON always thought she was a social worker and was constantly trying to run my department. Her suggestions were usually geared towards the medical model and designed to cover the nursing department's asses when they decided to trample on people's rights. There was not much a social worker, or anyone else can do for that matter, when it comes to nurses, even when they are wrong because, as said before, they are the elite group in nursing homes. Essentially this means, they are never, that's right, never wrong. It is harder to get a bad nurse in a nursing home fired, than it is to impeach a US President. A lot of this is because there is such a shortage of nurses in America that nursing homes take anything they can get, especially in a bad economy. The DON of a nursing home has to be a registered nurse, but these are not the four degree registered nurses we might think of. These registered nurses probably have taken an accelerated training course, at a community college that lasts maybe 2 years, if that. These registered nurses were LPN's who want a better pay scale. So the registered nurses in nursing homes are also not the best of the best.

Nursing assistants, sort of the backbone of any nursing home because they actually spend more time with the resident than nurses or even doctors do. If a loved one wants to know the real truth about what their loved one says or does, ask a nursing assistant, because they probably know more about a particular resident than their own family may know. This being said, amazingly enough, nursing assistants are treated like scum I nursing homes, especially by nurses and are almost never invited to care plan meetings. Care plan meetings are where relatives and staff and residents, if they choose to attend, discuss the resident's care, diet, etc. Why nursing assistants are not invited in a mystery to me, except for the fact they are treated like dirt. This, along with terrible pay, is likely the big factor why nursing assistants are no more the cream of society's crop than nurses are in a nursing home. In fact it is safe to say many are white trash thinking this will be an easy job. They think that until they are actually doing it and find out the job involves more than they anticipated. When the Welfare to Work Program was started a few years ago by the federal government, stipends were provided for nursing assistant and home health aide training courses for people to get off welfare. The pay is barely above minimum wage and this low wage does nothing to attract a higher plane of worker. This is not to say there are no good, dedicated nursing assistants, but the good ones are, unfortunately, the exceptions to the rule. If you ever wondered where nursing homes get a large share of its LPN nurses, they usually were nursing assistants who went to community college and wanted a higher pay scale. In fact, LPN courses usually only take 11 months, where Social Work and Sociology are four year degrees. I always thought it amusing that 11 month schooling nurses felt highly superior against a four year degreed program. All an LPN needs is a GED and 11 months of nursing school either at a local hospital or community college. Nursing assistants are the ones who take the brunt of a resident's aggressive behaviors such as punching, kicking and biting. It is a thankless job for the crappy pay and for all of the abuses and heavy lifting they must endure. Top all of this off with no consistent standards for training for nursing assistants across the state lines and in many states you are bound to get inferior care. For example; when I was a nursing assistant in NY State, I went through an 8 week course and felt like we were well trained. The course consisted of 4 weeks classroom training and 4 weeks, under an RN's supervision, on the floor, hands on training. When I worked as a Social Worker in Indiana, I found out their course consists of only 3 weeks in classroom and the LPN is supposed to finish training them on the job. Now remember the LPN is not exactly good at her job either.

Next up is the therapy department, who, much like nursing can also never do any wrong, even when they are wrong. Therapy is required for every single person, except those who are in a coma that reside in nursing homes. If a nursing home has a therapy department, it can, and does, bring in big bucks because therapy isn't cheap, folks by any means. This department and ever therapist in it, is the facility's cash cow, bringing in large amounts of money. The best part is therapy is Medicare reimbursed, so nursing homes can milk Medicare to the hilt.

There were many times when I did not always agree with therapy or nursing's decisions, especially when it came to residents' rights. Someone in therapy was always coming to my office to complain that a resident did not want to partake in therapy. I constantly explained to the therapists that I could point out the fact that if the resident refused for 3 days to not do therapy, Medicare would drop them.

Other than that, not much we could do because, by rights, the resident can refuse therapy. This always proved to be a mistake, even though Social Services are supposed to uphold a resident's rights. Therapy, nursing and, ultimately, the Administrator, felt Social Services should and must, find some way to over ride those rights, therefore bringing big money to the facility. The disagreeing with these entities, coupled with the facility hiring a back stabbing, opportunist for a Social Work assistant, was the beginning of my demise in this greedy little business. I learned the reason Social Workers usually do not stay in the same position for years, unlike the old days of nursing homes, is because the stress of always being at odds with what the facility wants (money over rides all else, come to find out) and what Social Workers are really supposed to do, which is to look out for the interests of the residents. The best interests of the residents are of little concern in a traditional nursing home because the bottom line, as in any business, is the important factor to stock holders, owners and the board of directors. Unfortunately the commodity or product here is human lives, which seems to be of little interest to business people.

The Activity Department did not command much respect when I first started working at St. Barley's because the Activity Director at the time was a pure flake. She would get all excited and flustered aver the dumbest things and end up looking stupid. She also did not want to do much as far as activities went, except the standard bingo fare, requiring little or no imagination. That particular Activity Director resigned after I was working at St. Barley's about a month. The new person who took the job was no more imaginative or ambitious, but I suppose her assistants were happy that anything was an improvement. The Activity Director had one of the former directors working part time as her assistant and consequently, unlike Social Services, never did any of her own paperwork or data entry. This Director of Activities turned out to be as lazy as the last one was but her assistants were happy to have anyone other than the former one because it seemed the last one did not get along with her assistants.

This one was on such a high plane that the Administrator assigned her to create Culture Change, which shows how ignorant of Culture Change the Administrator was. Culture Change is something that the entire staff of a facility has to make happen. It is not something that one department can simply pull off by itself. It shows how none of the department heads, or the Administrator understood one whit what Culture Change was or entailed. Any Culture Change that did take place was used strictly for marketing purposes and was not brought about because anyone cared about the residents' happiness at all. The Administrator was not the least bit interested in anything other than how to rake in money for the facility and nothing more, except keeping her ass out of a sling with state inspectors. Her demands, along with the ever present distrust of all department heads, made the work climate tense and inefficient. No matter what anyone said or suggested, it was not her ideas so they did not merit a second look. This woman wanted to control everything that went on, never allowing managers to fully run their own departments, and she stubbornly refused to be realistic. Her demands bordered on harassment whenever she would call one of the managers out in morning meetings to humiliate them in front of co-workers, mostly for daring to not run every single detail of everything past her first for approval. This woman was totally detached from the problems of her staff as well as any of the residents under her watch. Everyone detested her, except for those who falsely blew smoke up her ass to keep their jobs.

When I was a case manager for an outreach agency in Illinois, we were treated with respect because we brought in money for the agency, so we were considered essential to the company. In traditional nursing homes the Social Service department is considered a necessary evil by everyone. Traditional nursing homes, being based on the medical model, only considers people who are medical personnel to be essential. Social Work is merely tolerated by everyone in a traditional nursing home because we are looked upon as a department that brings in money. In a truly culture change environment, where all the staff works together, this is a different story. A person centered environment, like culture change is, considers the whole person and treats the residents as individuals, so their social, emotional wellbeing is important to the facility.

You can imagine my own culture shock when I worked traditional nursing homes and we, the social workers, were treated like the red headed step-child with freckles. We were openly shunned and treated with contempt by the medical and therapy staff and they didn't even try to disguise their disgust of us. Most traditional nursing homes do not really take the time to even understand what the Social Service department does, and could care even less about what our role is there. It is safe to say that most of the other workers saw us as merely the complaint department and not much more. Social Workers in a nursing home not only have to watch over, and spot any unusual behaviors of the residents, but we also noticed if a co-worker was experiencing burn out, which is a common problem with nurse aides, so there was a lot more to our role than they knew.

Showers Resemble a Car Wash

The matter of private rooms and showers and
bathtubs brings us to the barbaric concept of
the shared showers in nursing homes. Imagine
being a resident and it is shower time. The staff
makes the decisions about showering rituals,
such as times and how often you will get them.
Imagine it is 'time' for your shower; you are
placed in a chair on wheels made from white
tubular pipes. This sort of chair, where you are
usually stark naked, is cold and very sterile,
but, hey, it is easier for staff to keep clean,
so never mind your comfort. Staff can also
wheel it right over the toilet without having to
remove you from the chair, sort of like 'one stop
shopping.' This practice alone is barbaric and
is really where the warehousing affect kicks in

for residents in facilities. Staff tries their best to cover you, maybe they succeed and maybe your bare backside and bare back is showing as you are wheeled down a long, cold hallway to a community shower. This huge shower room is shared by every other resident who lives in the facility. You are wheeled into the community shower to be greeted by a hand held shower head on the end of a long hose. If you can shower yourself, you get to hold the device. If unable to do it yourself you will be soaped up, usually starting with your hair and drenched with the cascading water from the shower hose after being soaped from head to toe. All of this wonderful 'treatment' will be performed while you are still sitting in the cold, horrible chair on wheels made from plastic pipes. Well folks, this amounts to no more than a car wash for human beings. If I am fortunate enough to have my own soap products to keep my skin from drying out I get to use them.

If I am not that fortunate, I get to use industrial types of shampoo and soaps all created with no soft skin in mind at all. Industrial type soap is just what elderly people do not need at a time when their skin is becoming paper thin and with quite a bit of dryness setting in because they are older. Imagine having dementia and the world now appears scary to you and all of a sudden a waterfall of rushing water is blasted over your head. This would bring us right back to the 'behavior' section mentioned before. This kind of startling motion would trigger a behavior in even the best of us with our minds intact, much less a person with dementia. After being rinsed, I am still in this damned chair more than likely covered with goose bumps; the room is chilly because it is difficult to warm such a large room anyway. I am dried from head to toe, probably rubbing my delicate skin with scratchy towels after using industrial soaps. None of this is conducive to my well being, my delicate skin being able to heal, nor to being treated as a human being in general. Bathing and showers need to fit the residents' preferences. Bath times should be pleasant and scheduled around residents' choice of when and how often, not around a facility's schedule. All of this other stuff, as it is set up now in most facilities, is designed for efficiency, to run people through a human car wash and get the 'task' done as quickly as possible in an eight hour shift. This is not the kind of treatment I look forward to in a nursing home where I get to pay upwards of over $5,000 per month to live there. For $5,000 per month I could live in a grand hotel with room service and mints on my pillow and heated towels. Instead, I get to pay this huge amount to be treated like some piece of meat in a meat market.

Residents are seldom, if ever, in traditional nursing homes, asked if they prefer a shower or bath, except when they are admitted to the facility and usually only Social Services asked them because it is a question on our assessment sheet. I am sure staff never asked the resident and they certainly never asked my department. In fact, where I had worked, the tub was never used and when I inquired as to why, staff told me 'it just did not work anyway.' When I was an aide I gave many residents baths because I would ask. I will admit it took a little more time than wheeling someone into a shower, but residents loved the whirlpool tub very much. The tub also had a calming effect with residents who had dementia. There was just something about all those bubbles and the soothing warm water that most residents liked.

It is common for traditional facilities to only offer a shower or bath once or twice a week. I do not know how many of you only bathe once or twice per week, but to me this is ridiculous.

I understand older people have dryer skin, but still, offer more lotions then, but stop acting like people are cars to be run through a car wash.

A nursing home shower or bath should resemble a spa where people go to be pampered, not tormented in an ancient torture device straight out of the 16the century. I would like heated towels and maybe even soft music and a fireplace to help me relax. Even people with dementia can focus on a fireplace or soft music making it easier for staff to do their job if a normally combative resident is focused on something other than biting and kicking.

Sex and the Nursing Home Resident, a Taboo Subject

Nursing homes definitely are not places people think of anyone ever desiring sex, much less having any. More elderly, even in nursing homes, not only think about sex, they desire it but are usually deterred from thinking about it and definitely denied it, if staff has anything to say about it.

Most staff in nursing homes think older people having sex is disgusting and all old people who want sex must be perverts. It is expected that when old people enter a nursing home to live, they will automatically become eunuchs, understanding that sex was parked outside the doors and is a privilege only for the young, or at least, only for old people who live outside in the community. To nursing home staff, finding an empty room for people to engage in a sexual act, means having to clean a room that was already clean, and best left that way, in other words, more work for them. To corporations and owners, an empty room set aside for such purposes means a room not producing money 24/7 because it is empty.

This is almost like living in a concentration camp, minus the torture, unless you count the harsh words from staff as torture, maybe to some it is. Entering a nursing home means giving up all pleasures, except for those sanctioned by the facility. Perhaps there needs to be brochures that not only tell of the benefits of living in a nursing home, but also list the former pleasures you have to give up. Or maybe it would suit their marketing department if the brochure listed the pleasures sanctioned by the facility. Only things like bingo, reading is ok, looking out the window is fine, blah, blah, blah. I recall reading recently about a man whose wife is living in a nursing home, she has dementia and it appears that dementia enhances some people's sex drive. He appealed to the court to be able to have sex with his own wife because the nursing home refused to allow it. The judge ruled in favor of the nursing home, thus probably subjecting the wife to taking a psychotropic medication. Apparently a drugged person with dementia is preferable to allowing her to engage in sex with her husband. For some odd reason, nursing homes and courts think they must protect elderly from sex acts, especially if they have dementia. An older person with dementia is not the same as protecting a teenager or child from engaging in sex because they should not be exposed to sex until the age of consent. Most elderly people have lived their lives, are likely not virgins and therefore will not be traumatized by having sex. As things stand, if a person with dementia makes sexual advances towards a staff member because that person may remind them of their loved one, it is labeled a behavior and labeled as perversion. Usually if a staff member is kind but firm and sets down rules, the person with dementia will back off. It has been my experience that most staff people either delight in getting a resident in trouble, or are just pussies and refuse to handle any problems with residents on their own. Staff will usually like to have Social Services talk with the person who has dementia, which, by the way, several hours later has no meaning whatsoever because the person has forgotten about the incident due to memory problems. Or the staff likes Social Services to talk to family members, which in most cases is very embarrassing for them because the family may not understand the mechanics of the disease and how it works on some people. Wives and husbands especially usually get very embarrassed because they fear their loved one will get bad treatment or be thought of as a pervert.

Sex in nursing homes has long been a taboo

subject with staff because no one wants to think our parents or grandparents are interested in sex any longer. It is a totally ridiculous myth that old people never think about sex anymore when they have reached a certain age. It is so not true. I really doubt any of us will stop thinking about sex until we have taken our last breath. Sex is a natural part of life and if an elderly person has enjoyed a healthy sex life for many years, they should not be told it is wrong simply because staff has a problem with the idea. Staff had better get used to the new ideas because as Baby Boomers grow older and enter a nursing home, it is pretty likely they will bring their 1960's attitudes with them. Those attitudes meant sex with whomever they darn well pleased. It is becoming more obvious, from research being done and various books having been written that elderly people, not living in institutions, have sex. The old saying: "There may be snow on the roof, but there is still a fire in the fireplace" apparently rings truer than previously thought.

Doris a sweet 90 year old lady who had been at St Barley's for about two years liked to approach some of the men she thought were 'cute' as she liked to put it. Doris was in the habit of having a healthy sex life before coming to our nursing home and she 'missed the companionship of a man.' Doris was very alert and oriented and sharp as a tack. She also was still a very handsome woman, even at 90. She would sometimes try to get to know some of the gentlemen who came to St Barley's, either for a long-term stay or for therapy.

One Monday I returned to work and the DON approached me, red-faced, talking fast and acting almost frantic. "You have to have a talk with Doris right now" the DON said. She often liked to tell me I 'had to talk to someone, right now or immediately' without telling me why or what about. I asked her why I needed to talk to Doris and the DON said; "Because she has been acting cozy with Arthur and trying to hold his hand all weekend." I knew Arthur was not married and he had been a widower for well over 15 years, so Doris was not exactly acting all jiggy with a married man or anything. The DON said: "You have to tell her to stop it right this minute or we will call her daughter." "Arthur is not coherent; he has slight dementia and does not know what Doris is trying to do." I had to admit, from this scanty information, I did not know what she was trying to do either, except be very friendly with a gentleman. The DON told me I had to tell Doris there is no man in our facility that is with it enough to understand any sexual advances. I told the DON I would simply talk with Doris and try to get her side of the story. "What for?" she asked. "I have already told you what is going on." In the DON's opinion, I only needed her to tell me what is what and she felt like I did not trust her sole judgment, and frankly she was right, I did not. I could not take one side of a story, even from staff and not talk to the other person, it simply wasn't fair.

As I walked to Doris's room, I mulled over in my mind what to say. I knew I was going to ask her what was happening, in her words, and I kept thinking: "Do I say: 'Doris no man in his right mind wants your advances.' No that did not sound right, but neither did; 'No man is coherent enough to know what your advances mean.'

I found Doris in her room, sitting in the big chair next to the window. I said: "Doris, did something happen this past weekend?" "Why?" she asked. I explained to her the DON said some aides observed something that might be construed as inappropriate gestures toward Arthur. I said no one was accusing her of anything, but I needed to hear from her what went on that might possibly look like something more than an innocent hand holding. "It's that bitch of a head nurse, isn't it" she said. "I heard her talking at the nurse's station to an aide about it." I told her I wasn't at liberty to say who talked to me, but she shook her head. "You don't have to tell me, I already know it is her." "All I did was talk to Arthur, I swear and I did hold his hand during the movie in the lounge. Did I do something wrong?" She asked. I assured her that if that was the whole story, then no, she was not doing anything wrong.

I told the DON what Doris told me and she said she knew Doris was lying and I had to now call Doris's and Arthur's family and make out an incident report to the state so we did not 'get in trouble' for sexual abuse. I explained I did not see how sexual abuse had entered into this just by holding his hand. I also said I didn't think it appropriate to call both families to upset them. "Just do it" she said. She also said she was going to call the aide who was on duty over the weekend and ask her the true story. I was flabbergasted and did not understand why she felt the aide and herself were the only ones giving me the true story. I knew the DON was always over impressed with her position, but this was entirely ridiculous in my book. The DON gave a deep sigh and abruptly turned on her heel and walked away.

By late afternoon I was called into the Administrator's office and the DON was in one of the chairs in front of her desk. The Administrator motioned me to have a seat and I did. As soon as I sat down, the inquisition began. "Did you call Doris's and Arthur's families today?" she asked. "No, I said, I wanted to wait and try to get to the bottom of it all first. "You know we have to report all incidents of abuse as soon as possible" she told me. I explained I failed to see it as an abuse incident. I looked over at the DON, who was looking at the floor and refused to even look my way. She always did this crap when she knew she was getting someone into trouble. "Give her the new paper" the Administrator said to the DON. She handed me a new behavior sheet, she claimed she found, made out by the aide who was on duty over the weekend. I thought, sure you did, and took the new paper. The dates and time indicated it was written over the weekend, but it could have very well been fudged that day for all I knew. I looked at the paper which now stated that Doris had been observed, by the aide, rubbing Arthur's leg up to his groin area. Somehow the act went from holding his hand to rubbing his leg and groin. I seriously had my doubts, but I knew from experience there was no sense disputing this new evidence because the Administrator would always take the nurse's account as gospel. "You need to talk to Arthur and make sure he has not been traumatized by all of this" the Administrator told me. I wondered why they thought my talking to Arthur would do much good. If he did not understand the advances because of his dementia, how was he going to understand what I was asking him?

This was an innocent act that had gotten blown way out of proportion because the sex subject in this nursing home was so taboo, the nurse and aide were willing to get a resident in trouble over it. I was seething as I left the Administrator's office because she said she had to 'write me up' over not following through. I was pissed and when she asked me to sign the paper I refused to do it. This was just part of her trying to 'make a case' against me, trying to make me look incompetent so they might avoid a lawsuit. I was heading for 59 years old myself, not as cute and charming as the 25 year old young man they had in mind as my replacement, so in order to avoid being sued, they had to try to make me seem incompetent. Maybe the time they trumped up evidence, I was incompetent, because the DON and Administrator conveniently lost every single piece of paper I was giving them from then on. It would not matter to the Administrator if I had copies of those papers either, because she'd swear she never got them on time. They did not want an age discrimination suit, so trumping up evidence suited their purpose. What pisses me off about the whole thing is that a nursing home is the last place age discrimination should be going on. But this incident triggered a vendetta against me that I can only construe as age discrimination since I was not the ass kisser they wanted in my position. The older social worker the Administrator allowed to stay on was able to do so simply because the older lady was part time, a good friend of the owner and his wife, and they needed someone to man the front desk on weekends, because no one else would do it every single weekend, like she would. So they were using her pretty much anyway. The DON, already had made remarks at some of our meetings, about the older lady in Activities, who was a part time assistant there. The DON would look at her hand written care plans at our care plan meeting and say: "Her handwriting is getting pretty bad, because she is getting up there in age, I suppose." It is not a comforting thought when the DON really does not like older co-workers. Residents who are old are fine with her, they pay rent, but she made no bones about not liking older co-workers. She usually made disparaging remarks about how they just 'were slipping in their paperwork.'

None the less I left that office feeling totally undermined once again by the elite nursing group in this facility. My four year degree meant absolutely nothing to the DON or the Administrator, who, by the way, only possessed a GED herself. In Indiana, if you complete a six month internship with a licensed administrator, you are eligible to take an exam and become an administrator too, with nothing more than a GED or high school diploma.

If someone suffers from dementia, most adult children are under the impression their loved one does not fully understand what is going on. While most may not fully recall being teenagers and carefree with sex, it is doubtful having sex as an older person, will create the trauma adult children fear it will. It is not like older adults have never engaged in sex and there is no virginity to protect. Some medical research suggests a good dose of sex between two people who like each other, is in fact, good for their health and may improve a person's mood.

In my opinion, more adults need to have their lawyers draw up a sexual power of attorney so it isn't some big shock to family and loved ones if you want sex in your older years. Staff should be able to determine if it is safe for some people, but this would have to be on an individual basis. This decision should never be an OMG, no sex as some sweeping rule for all people. This is another issue where if someone, especially my children, God love them, tried to come to my house and tell me sex is over, would surely have a fight on their hands. So along with power of attorney for our assets and living wills, everyone should consider a sex power of attorney so no one is shocked, least of all institutions. Hey, play me some good 60's rock and roll, give me a soft light and let me go!!

Physical Therapy; a Bad Name

In nursing homes the term; 'physical therapy' is used, or 'music therapy' and 'speech therapy.' What's in a name? Plenty is in a name, if I decide to walk daily, it is called 'exercise' not physical therapy. In a normal, outside life, it is simply called exercising. Activity departments as well as the physical therapists should be using names like exercising and activity departments should offer walking exercises for anyone who wants to participate. Physical therapy and activities are decided by staff members of nursing homes, when the ultimate decisions of these activities should be resting with residents and their desires and wants. We all understand that physical therapy is necessary when a person has an injury, even younger ones, but it is a common notion among staff in nursing homes that residents are inherently lazy and will not get up on their own initiative to do any kind of activity, this is a wrong assumption. More residents would likely participate in activities of some sort if the right kinds of activities are offered. Here again, is where residents and families should be consulted concerning what they consider quality activities. If all nursing homes had vans, residents would probably enjoy going to the food courts at local malls and shopping, for many people this is a normal activity where they are being actively involved. Many nursing home residents sit around the hallways and nursing stations everyday when staff is not expecting state surveyors to come in. This is not an activity and residents look bored, those residents with dementia are confused and often ask where they should go or what they should do now. Even people with dementia are fully aware there are rules and regulations in nursing homes and are 'worried' they will 'do something wrong' like breaking a 'rule' by going someplace in the facility they think staff will consider 'off limits.'

Residents are woken up in traditional nursing homes, usually by 5:30 every morning. Why facilities get elderly people up so early is beyond me, they have no job to get to and have earned the right to sleep in, if they choose to do so. Where I worked, the staff would get residents up around five or five thirty and expect them to attend therapy sessions at nine in the morning. This schedule was strictly for therapy staff, which was considered the 'golden children' anyway because they brought in so much money. The therapy staff told me the early sessions were so they could fit everyone in before the end of the day. This therapy staff would, of course, make sessions available for people who lived in the community to come in at the end of a day, so I saw no reason to be making residents get up so early every day. The only reason therapy staff wanted those 'early' sessions was because they tried to cram as many people from the outside as they could in near the end of each day to make more money for the facility. I never understood why the full time resident was expected to make all the concessions for the facility. This, once again, brings us to the fact that a facility expects residents to conform to their routines, never requiring the nursing home to have to bend any. For a regimen like physical to be expected to enhance a person's quality of life, I do not see that end result when a person is required to show up at therapy very early in the morning if they do not want to. When therapists schedule people from the outside community, they always asked what time of day is more convenient for them. I see no reason why those people living in the nursing home should not be given any of the same courtesies of people in the community. This is a double standard in all its finest forms.

Physical therapy in a nursing home, like meals and everything else offered should be unhurried and socially rewarding. I have seen therapists complain to Social Services and even hand me a behavior sheet if a resident refused to attend the therapy. Therapists expected me to explain to residents that if they refused, three times in a row, their Medicare would drop them. I guess when one receives a nursing certificate or a therapist gets a degree, those pieces of paper render them unable to explain things to residents anymore. Or, if that is not the case, then I suppose those pieces of paper, unlike my degree, renders them the elite crowd who no longer has to lower themselves to a social worker's lowly status, to explain a damned thing to residents, even if they see that resident daily. I always thought it was peculiar just how those rules worked. Having each department explain what the Medicare rules are, having each department actually explain anything to residents that pertain to their department, costs nothing at all except the person's time, usually just a few minutes. So for each department to expect Social Services to do all of that for their department, simply amounts to pure laziness and nothing more. If Social Services in nursing homes were freed up from running interference for every damned department in a nursing home, thereby leaving time for social workers to do actual social work, would be cost effective as well.

Changes Any Nursing Home Can Make, if They Really Want to

A facility does not have to be a huge corporate giant to make the changes geared toward Culture Change. Buildings do not have to be totally renovated or rebuilt in order to initiate changes. In fact, physical changes are only cosmetic without an entire attitude change on the part of how a facility is run and Culture Change has no blueprint so every nursing home must decide just what will and will not work for their particular circumstance and for their residents.

The biggest change any facility can make, which costs no money at all, is to get rid of rules. Where I used to work, many times new residents, especially men, would ask us what the house rules were. I would have loved to tell them there are no rules, this is your home. Getting rid of rules does not mean a free for all and that residents can break the law. It does, however, mean a resident should be able to do what they are used to doing in their own home. Maybe not parade around naked in front of other residents, but also not the arbitrary rules so common to many nursing homes either.

Staff could carry remote pagers instead of the overhead pagers, like the place I last worked. Where I worked, overhead pagers would blast through the silence and startle every resident throughout the whole building. I do not have overhead pagers in my own home and I am sure none of the residents ever had any at home either. No one wants to hear a screeching voice blaring over an intercom system, especially during the night and afternoons if they are napping.

All staff in every nursing home should be cross trained because everyone is required to answer call lights to share in the care of the residents. I know how frustrating it was, when answering a call light, and I could not assist a resident to bed, to the bathroom, or assist in help with someone washing or changing. Staff was required to answer all lights, but if we were not certified as aides, it was absolutely useless, unless someone wanted nothing more than a drink of water or a magazine or a light turned on or off. I recall not being able to assist residents in anything major and going to get a nurse only to be brushed off because 'an aide was too busy.' This especially pissed me off because I know damned well nurses can assist a resident, so if one is just standing at the nurse's station doing nothing, they had damned well better get to whatever the resident needs. That was the epitome of elites in my eyes, a nurse who had likely once been an aide, now feeling too damned good to assist a resident. I remember wanting to slap those nurses so badly I saw red. If I am a resident needing to go to the bathroom, it is degrading to be made to wait.

Even if they wear briefs, it is degrading to leak or have an accident, plus it is not good for their skin to sit in urine or feces because some nurse was a lazy jerk. I would bring this up in meetings, only to be met with a brick wall because no one talks against a nurse, even when wrong, as afore mentioned. If all staff were cross trained, this could prove to be a big help for aides and for nurses, who may be very busy during certain times of the day.

Allow nursing assistants to make some on the spot type decisions without the micromanaging of every single, simple detail by nursing. If nursing assistant training were consistent and uniform from state to state, facilities could trust aides to make fairly good decisions on their own. As it stands now, a senior nurse aide can barely help a resident blow their noses without a clearance from nursing. In house, ongoing training for aides in every facility is not going to cost that much to ensure everyone is on the same page.

Another huge improvement would be the elimination of nurse's stations predominately placed in the middle of each wing right in everyone's way. Nursing stations placed this way only serves to amplify the fact the building is a medical facility, rather than anyone's home. Nurse's stations could be placed close to a hallway, in an office, but do not have to be in the main part of the wings. In traditional nursing homes, nursing stations have high counters, are obtrusive and so high no one in a wheel chair can see over them to talk to a nurse. A counter set up like this only creates the impression that nurses are above unapproachable or unfriendly and is not conducive to any sort of home like atmosphere that should prevail in all nursing homes. Nursing stations only reinforce the 'me against them' attitude residents may have toward staff to begin with. The nursing station also reinforces the institutional focal point in a nursing home, making people feel segregated. It is not home-like to have caregivers standing around a central nursing station waiting to answer call lights. The section that is now taken up by a nurse's station could be used as an open area where residents would find it much easier to maneuver in the hallways, especially wheel chair bound residents. The elimination of those damned nurse's stations could open up more space so the corners of the hallways could have comfortable end tables, comfortable chairs, radios and nice lighting for residents to sit and relax, perhaps enjoying tea or coffee.

In traditional nursing homes, when all hall ways lead to the central nursing station, I always had trouble getting around the halls in order to get to a person's room. This centralization of the hallways only makes for high traffic and congestions. It makes hallways a virtual obstacle course for residents, especially those in wheel chairs and with canes. It also ruins people's privacy because visitors often poke their heads in other people's rooms while going down the hallway. I don't have this going on in my private home.

There should be a time set aside each day for the residents to have a cocktail hour. This does not mean serving alcoholics cocktails to put them back on alcohol or serving alcohol to people who do not like it. Fruit juice combos can be served to those who do not want alcohol. There should be snacks served and residents should have this social hour every day to look forward to. But alcohol should definitely be served to those who can choose and who wish to have it. There can be a one or two drink minimum, if you like, but treat the elderly as adults.

Activities need to stop showing cartoon movies, unless residents request to see them.

There is nothing wrong with showing the latest comedy, even if there are sex scenes and swear words in them. I have no doubt that almost all of the residents in a nursing home have heard swear words at one time or another. One of the really tacky activities in our nursing home was the Senior Prom, put on by college students. It is commendable that college students wanted to come in and volunteer, but I noticed not one college guy showed up, not even the gay ones. This was put together by only college women who dressed up in some tacky gowns and served punch and played lame music from a CD. Not many residents showed up and many of those who did show up, left almost immediately grumbling. Since, where we worked, it was mostly college women who were running the Prom, all it did was serve as a dating game fest for my young, male assistant, who ran out to introduce himself. We had many activities put together by older people in the community and I assure you, my assistant did not jump on those opportunities to run out and introduce himself to those promoters and his display was disgusting.

Residents have an organization in nursing homes called; resident council to be able to discuss with staff members the things that could be done to improve every nursing home. In resident council meetings, every department head should be present, at least once a month, to understand what the residents want to see changed, in their favor. Certainly an administrator needs to be present at every single meeting, simply because usually, the administrator is the one single person who can actually see to it that those changes are carried out.

The facility where I worked last had one of those organizations, except the Administrator and the DON always felt they were above having to sit in on any of the meetings. Administrators should be sitting in on every single resident council meeting because the discussions are about change. Where I worked, the Administrator always wiggled out of this responsibility and wanted the Activity Director to take notes and report back to the Administrator. This notion was totally ridiculous because the only person capable of getting any changes done is the Administrator. If the Administrator sat in on each one, then the ideas could be addressed immediately, not two weeks or even two months later, when staff brings it to their attention.

Most of the time the warning to the Activity Director from the Administrator, was to 'not allow the meetings to turn into a bitch session.' This attitude, on the part of any staff, is appalling and demeaning to residents. This attitude clearly sent the message to everyone that the Administrator could have given a damn about what residents needed or wanted.

Facilities also have Quality Assurance meetings and where I worked, no resident or family members were ever invited. I fail to understand how any quality improvements could possibly be made or decisions of what needs to be done could be made without input of people who live there, not people who go home to the outside every single day. I don't think I would want anyone coming to my home telling me what improvements were to be done without my giving some sort of input. Family members and residents should be welcomed by nursing home administrators as part of the facility's care team. Staff has no business sitting around a big, impersonal conference table making residents' decisions in the first damn place. This practice gives residents no face and no voice as to how their home is to be run. Any facility that truly cares for their residents will be concerned enough about the satisfaction level of those in their care and will be willing to make the necessary adjustments. Nursing homes should all be using surveys as a good instrument for what residents and families really want and it is a good instrument for reflection, if a facility really uses it well, of how the nursing home is doing, as far as performance, in the eyes of their consumers. Believe me, perception, on the part of any consumer, is everything, as far as understanding trends that people want and expect to see. A good survey is an important instrument for any company to use.

I have noticed, even in the better nursing homes, there is sometimes, a sentence that may say 'visiting hours are' well, there are no visiting hours in my home. Adult children loved ones and friends are going to worry about their loved ones, and even much more so once that loved one is in a nursing home. If my loved one wants to come see me at 11PM in my home, it is up to me, not an administrator, if they can come in at that hour or not. Sure, I lock my doors at 10PM, maybe and residents need to be kept safe. But all nursing homes must, then, have a bell to allow visitors to ring the bell, identify themselves and be allowed in, there are no two ways about this subject. If my parent or grandparent is residing in a nursing home, you damned well better be letting me in when I come calling, unless I am causing a disturbance, which is a far out scenario anyway.

When visiting a nursing home, look, or ask if there is a ''visitor's policy' in place for certain hours, I say the answer better be 'no' or I am saying no to this nursing home and looking elsewhere for my loved one to live. It is not a hospital it will be your loved one's home. If there is a visiting hour policy, I have no idea what planet the administrator landed on earth from then.

Observe and even interview, the workers. In many traditional nursing homes, especially with bad management, the workers are not happy. If workers do not like the place, the chances are pretty good my loved one will not like it either. Culture change helps to keep workers happy, which means a facility saves money because it costs money to have to replace workers. If the workers are going out the door like smoke, a facility better be looking at why this is. If workers are happy it is far more likely the residents will be happy and this makes for a lot less complaining from families as well. With happy staff, happy residents comes better survey results and less need for marketing because if a place is making people happy, there will be a long list of residents wanting to live there. Happier workers, happier residents and happier families also help result in less burnout for workers. Burnout usually results from too many demands on workers, especially nursing assistants and nurses.

While visiting ask if relatives and residents are invited to meetings held concerning how money is spent, how the policies are created, etc. If the answer is no then ask them why not. If you are concerned about this sort of thing, let the administrator know this right up front.

Culture Change and Competitiveness/ Conclusion

In view of the new Medicare cut backs, it is my theory that Medicare wants the most bang for the buck. In many ways this is good because while some nursing homes will close their doors, I believe it may be good that the inferior ones will be weeded out, so to speak. In order to be competitive, nursing homes will find the list for people who actually want to live there will be long. Most people will flock to a facility that resembles their home, not some hospital. It's true, it will be hard for the elderly to maybe have to move, but moving to a nursing home that treats the right is a plus, not a bust. Certainly I have seen nursing homes forcing residents move anyway, for the nursing home's convenience, so it is not as if residents have not been forced to move before, it is just that, maybe now, the moves will be for the better, for the improvement of their welfare and not at the whim of nursing home staff.

It is a good thing, maybe, that Medicare has now decided to stop simply handing out reimbursements to every corporate and privately owned facility calling itself a nursing home. This just may be the ticket to force nursing homes to have to change their ways and take a renewed look at the changes to make them more competitive, this can be a good thing. Elder care has become increasingly more competitive, like any other business. Baby Boomers are not willing, like the generation before them that was willing to simply conform and settle for rules and regulations of the ancient facilities. It's time for a change and perhaps Medicare will be the catalyst to usher in some of those changes. Hopefully this cut back effort will mean the state and federal surveyors will now revamp the entire system and check lists they now use to judge the performances of a really good nursing home.

While working in a nursing home I already knew the MDS, the instrument nursing homes and Medicare use to be able to justify the Medicare reimbursement money, was being redesigned to implement big changes. The changes are to, hopefully, make the MDS less generalized, sort of one size fits all mentally, to reflect much more individuality for each resident. This is supposed to reflect a single resident's personal challenges and needs much more than generic criteria that have been used, in my opinion, far too long to deliver good services to our nation's elderly population. Maybe the new Medicare cut backs will help keep more nursing homes honest. For far too long many facilities have, in my opinion, used Medicare to cheat the federal government out of tax monies, simply because the nursing home was able to slap a nursing home sign on their doors. Maybe this will also force facilities to have to train their nurse aides better to be able to deliver better services, since nurse aides have always been the primary care givers there. It is a popular belief, in traditional nursing homes, that treating people like humans with rights and with dignity, must be more expensive, not true. If money were the only answer, then residents in a nursing home would be treated like kings and queens and be living in a palace. I have seen the money Medicare and residents pump into nursing homes, money that lines the pockets of a CEO or a COO and buys corporate mansions complete with swimming pools and expensive vacations. I have seen it even buying huge meeting halls and fabulous buildings called corporate offices. But I have not seen it buying a wonderful final chapter in the lives of the older people who have made the corporate head's life wonderful. Are the corporate heads the only ones entitled to a nice life, a life provided for them by riding the backs of older American's miseries? I have seen the big money that buys the heads of pharmaceutical companies the same luxuries. I have seen a pharmacy charging older people, especially in a nursing home, $100 per pill simply because it is in the pharmacy's best interest to prolong a life that pays $100 per pill and residents are forced to use the in-house pharmacy. These are older people, who as a captive audience, have to sign agreements to buy medicine, while in the nursing home, from the company pharmacy because it is simply their policy under the guise that it is for the old person's own good to do so, or that a corporation has their best interest at heart. Traditional nursing homes are places where misery and despair come home to roost like chickens in early evening on a farm. People go to war these days and are called heroes, yet once they too are old, all of that will be forgotten until a few shovels of dirt cover their coffins and if they are lucky, when old, they will be able to live life out in their own homes, but probably not.

I look around a traditional nursing home and I see an old man slumped in a chair, a man whose parents probably once loved him and nurtured him. A man who probably loved his children and nurtured them, who now needs some assistance with everyday tasks that we, in our younger years, take for granted. What is the message a traditional nursing home is saying? I see the message as: "I am sorry old age has robbed you of being able to care for yourself and now, in this facility, we will continue to rob you as well. We will rob you of the dignity of making any decisions for yourself, of being able to choose when to eat, what to eat and when to go to bed, when to go outside and when to go to the bathroom and if it is not convenient for us, or fits into our schedule, you will wait. And, most of all, we will continue to rob you of any money we can get, because you were busy trying to pay bills or raise a family and did not save up a few million dollars to hire help in your own home. You do, however, have the privilege of paying for this lifestyle, the lifestyle we choose for you."

I suppose it would not be right, in this politically correct society, to make a movie about nursing home life. I suppose it would ruin those pretty brochures that corporations spend so much money on, the ones showing only smiling residents with an arm of some staff member draped over their shoulders. The pretty brochures, paid for by charging residents so much. Money spent on brochures instead of spent on making the facility more like a home. We, as nursing home staff, are sent to training on how to handle the difficult resident and their family, on how to handle behaviors, on how to not get sued, but rarely on how to develop culture change, or how to get rid of the rules in a nursing home. Rules that everyone, over the years, has simply and blindly, accepted as this is just how it is run. Just because a rule is written, or in place, or is a corporate policy, does not make the rule good or right.

I remember many students, about to graduate college, saying: "I don't think college has prepared me for work, has taught me everything I need to know." I know they are right. College only teaches the basics, young students who have only lived with Mom and Dad do not know about the plight of elderly people in nursing homes. It is rare we talked about it in any class, except to talk about the concept of Medicare and Medicaid, two programs that do not work well enough for the federal government, does not make money for officials. But students will find out soon enough, if they work in traditional nursing homes, about programs for a group of people who only represent a 'bottom line' for corporations and private owners of nursing homes.

Maybe schools do not want to teach people the truth about nursing homes for fear of scaring them all away. Most young Social Workers talk about 'working with families or youth' but hardly ever with the elderly. Geriatrics courses are few and far between and usually only offered as electives and not mandatory, like classes concerning youth and women in poverty or family dynamics are.

How to Judge a Nursing Home

Medicare has a web site with a nursing home checklist on it to try and help people who are looking for a good facility to use as a basis for this search. Lately there has been a lot of talk concerning the star rating of nursing homes as well. While both of these criteria have some merit, I say neither one goes far enough. Finding a good facility is still, at best, a complicated issue. I am hoping this book and this checklist will help people to understand more about how to judge a good facility.

The Medicare checklist says:

Basic information: My comments are in Italics:

1) The nursing home is Medicare-certified. This is very important especially from a financial standpoint. Medicare will not cover needed therapies if it is not a certified facility. *Hell, I say, also be sure the facility is licensed by the state it is in to operate legally. This may sound fundamental and crazy in this day and age, but some places have been known to operate illegally. Ask to see their state license.*

2) Be sure the nursing home is Medicaid-certified. *See the above comments, they cover this as well.*

3) Be sure the nursing home has the level of care you need (e.g. skilled, custodial), and a bed is available. Skilled nursing or (SNF) means that a facility is capable of providing skilled nursing care, which means proper medical care for people needing medical care, which means rehabilitation care as well.

4) The nursing home has special services if needed in a separate unit (e.g. dementia, ventilator, or rehabilitation), and a bed is available. *Before touring a nursing home and wasting your time, always ask if there are any available beds. Nothing is more disappointing than taking a tour, liking the place only to be told there is no room right now. Not all facilities have dementia units either, so inquire about this and then tour the dementia units to see how they are run. It appears lately that surveyors have been known to give facilities with dementia units a hard time about residents wandering. People with dementia sometimes tend to wander, so be sure the unit has a safe place for your loved ones to wander, if need be.*

5) The nursing home is located close enough for friends and family to visit. *This one is good, but in today's mobile society, family may not*

always live near the facility. Be sure then that the facility does not mind if you call, day or night, to be able to ask anything you like about your loved one. The staff works for your loved one, not the other way around. If they seem curt or rude when you call, consider another facility if this bothers you.

Resident Appearance

1) Residents are clean, appropriately dressed for the season or time of day and well-groomed. *This one may seem basic but it is very important. Be sure your loved one is able to wear the comfortable clothes you have sent to them or they have brought with them. Be sure their hair is in a style to your liking as well. I have seen some hideous hairdos on residents either because the staff didn't take time to fix the hair properly or because some staff member decided to*

change the hairdo to what they liked

on a person. The not having time to fix

the hair properly is a big one. It may

indicate the staffs' time is stretched too

far, too many people to care for. Not a

good sign. Inquire about this if it makes

you uncomfortable. Also take this one

step further and be sure residents are not

just sitting around the halls, slumped in

their chairs. Observe to be sure residents

are in some sort of activity, even if that

activity is simply looking out the window.

Be sure residents do not appear to be

disengaged from their surroundings.

Nursing Home Living Space

1) The nursing home is free from
    overwhelming unpleasant odors.
    This is another basic thing to look
    for. Take this one a step further
    by asking to see the tub room and

shower area, if no one is using them. Ask if the whirlpool tub is used and how often. Ask how often a resident gets a shower or bath. I can tell you that once a week, for me, doesn't cut it. I don't care if the answer is: "But we do sponge bathe in between." At home, I shower daily. Also ask what time your loved would have to get up in the morning. No resident should have a mandatory time of 5 or 6 AM simply for staff convenience. Be sure your loved will be allowed to sleep in until they decide to get up.

2) The temperature in the nursing home is comfortable for residents. *I won't touch this one because temperature is an individual choice.*

3) The nursing home has good lighting. *This goes without saying, but harsh,*

bright lights over a resident's bed
is also for staff convenience. Be
sure to look at overhead lighting in
your loved one's room to be sure it
is within reach and bright enough so
residents do not trip because they are
in the dark.

4) Noise levels in the dining room and
   other common areas are comfortable.
   Look at where your loved one will be
   eating. Assess it and ask yourself if
   it looks like an area where you would
   want to eat. No dining room should
   look and be set up like some military
   mess hall. Also inquire about what is
   served and if everyone has a choice.
   If the choice is too limited to what
   is served that day, consider another
   facility that is more accommodating
   to individual's preferences. Inquire

about snacks and be sure they aren't limited to hospital fare like a small package of graham crackers and the like. This type of choice will tell you, in an instant, that the facility is being cheap. Be sure your loved one can have the snacks they want, not some snacks strictly set up by a dietitian. Drop in at meal times and see if the dining room set up is to your liking.

5) Smoking isn't allowed or may be restricted to certain areas of the nursing home. *Now I am not going to say smoking is good, but it is legal. If a person has smoked for most of their life, a facility should accommodate this. Enough said.*

6) Furnishings are sturdy, yet comfortable and attractive. *Be sure all the furniture is not some cookie*

cutter mentality either. Enough said here too.

Staff

1) The relationship between the staff and the residents appears to be warm, polite and respectful. *Observe to see if residents know their aides personally, those who have been there a long time especially. Ask what the ratio of staff to residents is to your liking. With culture change, the ratio is smaller than 8 to 1 and be sure to ask if the same aides care for your loved one daily because if staff moves around too much they cannot possibly know what you and your loved one wants.*

2) All staff wears name tags. *This one is debatable because if the*

*ratio of staff to resident is small
and the same aides are assigned
to your loved ones, name tags
would be unnecessary. To be
truly home, let's face it, people
we meet in the world do not wear
name tags. This is too much like
an institution for me.*

3) Staff knocks on the doors before
   entering a resident's room and
   refers to residents by name. *This
   is very important because no one
   gets into my home unless they
   knock and identify themselves.
   Also don't let staff get away with
   elder speak like: "Honey, sweetie
   or baby or dear," instead of
   names. This is so disrespectful to
   me.*

4) The nursing home offers a

training and continuing education program for all staff. *This is important especially since, like I said, rules vary from state to state about training requirements. Don't be afraid to ask what kind of education is offered to staff. Like I also said, it could be: "How to deal with difficult residents and their families." With culture change there would be a lot less difficulties to deal with.*

5) The nursing home does background checks on all staff. *This is very important too because the facility I worked at was fined thousands of dollars because one nurse did not have a current license. In fact, her license had*

been revoked. No one bothered to check, it took a state surveyor to find this error.

6) The guide on your tour knows the residents by name and is recognized by them. *This is important for Administrators. Never trust an administrator who never leaves his/her office and residents much less families even know who they are or what they look like. Where I worked, when the administrator did leave her office, I was shocked to see her. The woman only left her office, in the two years I worked there, maybe three or four times. Not good. Always ask to meet the administrator and be sure to ask them critical questions to know*

how well they know their own facility. Ask them questions until you are comfortable with the answers.

7) There are licensed nursing staff 24 hours a day, including a Registered Nurse (RN) present at least 8 hours a day, seven days a week. *Where I worked, the facility was cited for not having an RN on duty on weekends.*

8) The same team of nurses and Certified Nursing Assistants (CNA) work with the same residents four or five days a week. *This sounds nice but rarely happens in traditional nursing homes. This is where culture change comes in. Nursing Assistants should have*

❧

a permanent assignment of residents, so should nurses. Also ask if the aide will be attending any care plan meetings. If not, find out why.

9) Certified Nursing Assistants work with a reasonable number of residents. We have gone over this and the reasons why.

10) Aides are involved in care plan meetings. *Unless there is culture change in a facility, it is seldom, if ever, that aides are invited to the meetings. Aides know your loved one better than most nurses do. Ask why they aren't present if they do not attend care plan meetings.*

11) There is a full time social worker on staff. *This is my favorite, for obvious reasons. Also ask if he/*

she is expected to do any other job like admissions or marketing. If the answer is yes, this is not good as I mentioned already in this book. If there are more than 100 beds in the facility, be sure the social worker has an assistant to help.

12) There is a licensed doctor on staff who is there daily and can be reached at all times. *Good luck with this one. It looks good on paper, but being there daily and reached at all times seldom happens in traditional facilities.*

13) The nursing home's management team (including the Director of Nursing and the Administrator) has worked together for at least one year. *Good luck on this one*

too. This was also talked about earlier in this book. Read it and take it from there.

Residents' Rooms

1) Residents may have personal belongings and/or furniture in their rooms. *This is important, but I personally would not place my loved one in a two person room with a perfect stranger as mentioned in this book.*

2) Each resident has storage space (closet and drawers) in his or her bedroom. *Remember the 9 inch rule? Be sure a facility isn't obsessed with such ridiculous rules.*

3) Each resident has a window in his or her bedroom. *There is more to it than this. I'd want my loved one to have* a private *room so he or she has access to the window at all times. If my loved one likes fresh air, a private room insures there is no big conflict with a roommate.*

4) Residents have access to a personal telephone and television. *Some places charge extra for cable hookups and some do not. Some places, the cable is included at no extra charge. Always inquire to what their policy is. Same goes for telephones. As Baby Boomers*

age, they may also want a
plug for their laptops.

5) Residents have a choice of
roommates. *Now we all know
how I feel about roommates.
But if my loved one wanted
a roommate, and some do,
make sure they have a choice.
Many facilities will say: "This
is all we have available right
now, but if it doesn't work out
we can change it." This may
or may not prove to be true.
So if this is the answer, only
you and your loved one can
decide if this is acceptable or
not.*

6) Water pitchers can be reached
by residents. *Also be sure,
when you visit each time to*

see if water is always in the pitcher, preferably fresh water. Ask your loved one if this is the case always.

7) There are policies and procedures to protect residents' possessions. *Many times facilities will say they discourage people from bringing in anything valuable or money. Inquire if they have a safe and what the hours are to access the safe. This is a person's home they should have access to items and money in their homes when they choose.*

Hallway, Stairs, Lounges and Bathrooms

1) Exits are clearly marked.
   The reasons for this should be obvious.

2) There are quiet areas where the residents can visit with friends and family. *This is pretty obvious too. But in a culture change facility, with private rooms, this would not be a concern.*

3) The nursing home has smoke detectors and sprinklers. *This one, I believe, is a state law everywhere. If concerned, ask what their disaster plan is. In Louisiana when hurricane Katrina hit, at least one nursing*

❀
271

home decided not to evacuate the residents and they all drowned. The administrator, of course, didn't drown. Be sure the disaster plan isn't "I'll save my own ass," plan. Not that anyone would admit it is, but in case of a disaster, you will want to know where they evacuate residents to in case you need to find your loved one.

4) All common areas, resident rooms and doorways are designed for wheelchair use. *This one is common sense if a facility takes wheelchair*

*bound residents. I would
be sure too, if my loved
one is in a wheelchair,
there are no high shelves
in the closet that a person
in a wheelchair can't
possibly reach.*

5) There are handrails in the
hallways and grab bars
in the bathrooms. *This is
standard safety and if they
don't exist, there is truly
something wrong here.*

References

Cunningham, Janet A., M.D., M.P.H. and Gurvich, Tanya, Pharm. D.

(2000). Published by The American Academy of Family Physicians.

Appropriate Use of Psychotropic Drugs in Nursing Homes.

Web site: http://www.aapp.org

CMS. Centers for Medicare & Medicaid Services. Web site: http://www.cms.hhs.gov. Retrieved December, 2009.

EAR Foundation. Seniors Fear Loss of Independence, Nursing Homes More Than Death. Web site: http://www.marketingcharts.com/direct/seniors-fear-loss-of-independence-nursing-homes-more-than-death-2343/. Retrieved from Internet, June, 2009.

Hutt, Jabba. Fictional character in George Lucas's Star Wars Movie. http://en.wikipedia.org/wiki/Jabba_the_Hutt Retrieved from Internet, March, 2010.

Johnson, Carla, AP Medical Writer. Minn. teen girls charged in nursing home abuse. Web site: http://www.foxnews.com December 4, 2008. Retrieved from Internet on April 17, 2009.

Murphy, Audie. Actor. Born 1921. Died 1971.

http://en.wikipedia.org/wiki/Audie_Murphy

Retrieved from Internet, March, 2010.

Nintendo Wii is a product of the Nintendo
Corporation. All rights reserved.

Biography

Roberta Weathers is from the Finger Lakes area of New York State. She has a Bachelors degree in Sociology and a Master's degree in Organizational Management. She has worked with the older population for over twenty years in different capacities, first as a nursing assistant then as a home health aide and also as a Social Services Director in a long term care facility.